LEARN TO CROCHET

LEARN TO CROCHET

SUE WHITING

CRE▲TIVE
ARTS & CRAFTS™

An imprint of CREATIVE HOMEOWNER, Upper Saddle River, NJ

First published in the United States and Canada in 2004 by

An imprint of Creative Homeowner®
Upper Saddle River, NJ
Creative Homeowner® is a registered trademark of Federal Marketing Corp.

Current printing (last digit) 10 9 8 7 6 5 4 3 2 1
Library of Congress card number: 2003112174
ISBN: 1-58011-176-9

Senior Editor: Clare Sayer
Production: Hazel Kirkman
Design: Frances de Rees
Photographer: Shona Wood
Editorial Direction: Rosemary Wilkinson

Reproduction by Pica Digital PTE Ltd, Singapore
Printed and bound by Times Offset (M) Sdn. Bhd., Malaysia

CREATIVE HOMEOWNER
A division of Federal Marketing Corp.
24 Park Way
Upper Saddle River, NJ 07458
www.creativehomeowner.com

CONTENTS

INTRODUCTION

Crochet is a relaxing and rewarding craft and is surprisingly easy to do – all you need is a ball of yarn and a crochet hook and you're on your way.

Once the first few basic stitches are mastered, all the textured and lacy effects are simple to achieve because they are just combinations of the basic stitches. It's the way the stitches are placed and combined that creates the stunning effects. And once you've learned how placing the stitches affects the finished look, everything else is easy.

Crochet is portable too. Because you never have more than one stitch on your hook at any time, there's no risk of "dropping stitches." Crochet hooks are much shorter than most knitting needles, so your crochet work can be easily tucked into your handbag, ready to pull out whenever you're on a long car trip, waiting for an appointment, or watching TV.

There are very few limits to what you can create in crochet. You can make new "antique" pieces of lace using the classic crochet cotton or create stunning textural multi-colored jackets and throws using any of many fabulous hand-knitting yarns. And remember, you don't have to use crochet to create the whole item. Try livening up a tired sweater with a border crochet trim or add patch pockets with a couple of "granny squares."

Once you've mastered the basics, let your imagination run wild and you'll soon be creating your own unique crochet masterpieces!

Sue Whiting

Basic Information

Crochet is surprisingly simple and does not require a lot of special equipment – all you need is a ball of yarn and a crochet hook, and you're ready to go. Once you have assembled your materials, there are some basic terms you will need to understand before you begin.

Crochet hooks

Crochet hooks come in a variety of sizes. The smallest crochet hooks are generally made of steel and are used for very fine lace work using yarns not much thicker than sewing thread. Thicker hooks are made of aluminum, and the really big chunky ones, used mainly for very thick yarns, are often made of plastic. Some of the aluminum ones have plastic handles – this makes them more comfortable to hold.

In this book, US sizes are given for all crochet hooks – use this chart to find the equivalent metric or imperial (old UK) size.

US	Metric	Old UK
-	0.60 mm	6
-	0.75 mm	5
-	1.00 mm	4
-	1.25 mm	3
-	1.50 mm	2½
5 steel	1.75 mm	2 or 15
B/1	2.00 mm	14
-	2.25 mm	13
C/2	2.50 mm	12
-	3.00 mm	11
D/3	3.25 mm	10
E/4	3.50 mm	9
F/5	3.75 mm	-
G/6	4.00 mm	8
7	4.50 mm	7
H/8	5.00 mm	6
I/9	5.50 mm	5
J/10	6.00 mm	4
K/10½	6.50 mm	3
-	7.00 mm	2
-	8.00 mm	0
-	9.00 mm	00
-	10.00 mm	000

Yarns for crochet

You can use almost any yarn for crochet. There are fine-gauge crochet cottons available that are generally for delicate lace work using the equally fine steel crochet hooks. Most hand-knitting yarn is ideal for crochet. Simply match the hook size to the thickness of the yarn. As a rough guide, when you are crocheting with a hand-knitting yarn, use a crochet hook in a size that corresponds with the yarn's recommended knitting needles.

While you can crochet with almost any hand-knitting yarn, there are certain types of yarn that will be slightly more difficult to use. Obviously a bouclé yarn will not be as easy to loop through and a yarn that is loosely twisted can cause you to split the threads as you work. If you are in any doubt as to whether a yarn will work for crochet, try making a swatch before you begin, or consult your local yarn store for advice.

Other equipment

In addition to a pattern, hook, and yarn, you will want to have a few other items on hand before you begin.

A tape measure is essential for measuring both the gauge of the work and the size of the pieces. (See "Gauge," below.)Lay the work flat to measure it, avoiding the temptation to gently stretch it to the desired size.

For darning in ends and sewing seams, you will need a blunt-pointed needle with an eye large enough to thread with the crochet yarn. Tapestry needles and yarn needles are ideal.

You will also need a pair of scissors to cut the yarn – small embroidery scissors are a good choice. And if you need to pin pieces together for any reason, use long bead-headed pins or T-pins that will hold the pieces securely and will not get lost in the work as easily as ordinary dressmaking pins.

Details of anything else you may need to complete the piece, such as buttons,
elastic, or ribbon, are usually given with the pattern.

Pressing or blocking

Once your crochet work is completed you may need to press it. (See page 48.) Check the pressing instructions given on the ball band of your yarn and adjust the heat of your iron accordingly. As a general rule, you should avoid pressing on the right side, and cover your work with a clean cloth.

Gauge

The size of your finished item will be determined by the size of each crochet stitch. The term used to describe this is the "gauge." Establishing the proper gauge is probably the most important step and well worth the effort it takes. Each crochet pattern will give details of the gauge you need to achieve to ensure your item is the required size and, where there are pieces that need to be joined

BELOW: Apart from your crochet hook and yarn, you will need a few basic items: pins, scissors, needles and a tape measure.

together, that everything will fit together correctly. It is important that you work to the proper gauge. If you do not, the item will not hold its shape properly and you may run out of yarn. The gauge is generally given as a number of stitches and rows that need to be achieved within a certain measurement, usually 4 inches. Sometimes the gauge will indicate the required size of one motif, or the first few rounds of something circular.

Before you begin to make the item, take time to check your gauge by working a gauge swatch. If the gauge is given over 4 inches, crochet a 5-inch square using the stitch pattern for that design. Once the swatch is completed, mark out 4 inches in both directions and count the number of stitches and rows you have achieved. If you have more stitches and rows than given in the gauge paragraph, you are working too tightly. This means that your item will be too small and the fabric may be too stiff. Try again using a larger size hook. If you have too few stitches and rows, your work is too loose, the item will be too big, you may run out of yarn, and the item will be floppy and not hold its shape. Again, work another swatch, this time using a one-size smaller hook. Continue making swatches until you match the gauge of the pattern exactly.

When you have achieved the correct gauge, use this hook to work the design. Where a pattern uses several hook sizes, you will have to adjust all of the hooks in the same way. If you achieve the proper gauge on a hook that is one size smaller, use one size smaller hook than stated throughout the pattern.

Sizes

Most of the projects in this book are in just one size. Where designs are in more than one size, the pattern is written for the smallest size with the variations needed for the larger sizes in square brackets [ ]. Where there is only one set of figures given, it applies to all sizes.

Work the figures in round brackets ( ) the number of times stated after the second bracket.

Abbreviations

Crochet patterns are not written out in full because it would simply take up too much space. Instead, they are written in a shorthand that abbreviates each crochet term. Use this list of standard crochet abbreviations for all the projects in this book.

beg	beginning
ch	chain
cont	continue
dc	double crochet
dec	decreas(e)(ing)
foll	following
hdc	half double crochet
inc	increas(e)(ing)
MS	main shade
patt	pattern
rep	repeat
RS	right side
sc	single crochet
sp(s)	space(s)
ss	slip stitch
st(s)	stitch(es)
tr	treble
WS	wrong side
yo	yarn over

Sometimes when a design uses a special stitch or group of stitches, you will find an abbreviation for this term given with the pattern.

Yarn quantities

The quantities of yarn you will need to make the item will be given with the pattern, but this is usually based on average requirements. If you decide to make the item slightly larger or smaller, you will need more or less yarn. And if your gauge is wrong, you may have a lot of yarn left over or you may run out. Because the color of a yarn can vary slightly between dye lots, buy all of the yarn you'll need to complete the project at the same time. This way all the balls or skeins carry the same dye lot number.

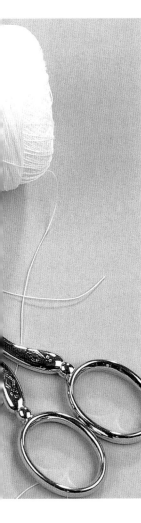

The First Stitches

Once you have chosen your yarn and selected your crochet hook, you are ready to begin. Here are the most common and frequently used stitches in crochet.

THE SLIP KNOT

All crochet begins with a slip knot. Unlike knitting, there is only one stitch on the hook at any time and the slip knot is the starting point for all of the stitches that go to make up the finished work.

1. When you make the slip knot, use the cut end of yarn to tighten the loop. Slip this loop over the crochet hook, and pull up the end so the loop sits comfortably around the crochet hook, just below the actual hook section (**A**). The resulting loop on your hook is your first stitch.

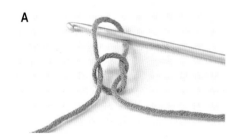

A

STARTING TO CROCHET

There are many different ways to hold the crochet hook and the yarn, but the right way is the way you find most comfortable and easiest.

Hold the hook in your right hand and the yarn in your left hand, feeding the yarn from the ball with your middle finger and holding the completed stitches between thumb and

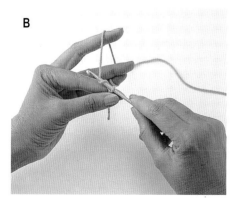

B

forefinger, just below the working stitch (**B**). Remember to hold the yarn at an even tension so that each stitch is of the same size.

CHAIN

Almost all crochet begins with a long chain of simple stitches that are used as the foundation for the rest of the work. These stitches are called "chain" stitches (**abbreviated to "ch"**) and the starting string is called the "foundation chain."

1. To make a chain stitch, wrap the yarn around the hook, bringing it up from the back, over the hook and taking it back to the back below the hook (**C**). Now gently pull this loop of yarn through the loop already on the hook to make the first chain stitch. Remember to use the yarn end that runs to the ball for the stitches or else you will run out quickly.

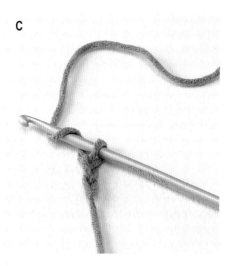

C

2. Continue wrapping the yarn over the hook (**abbreviated to "yo"**) and drawing new stitches through until you have the required number of chain stitches. It is quite easy to count the stitches: along the chain there will

be one neat "V" for each chain stitch (**D**). Don't count the slip knot as a stitch.

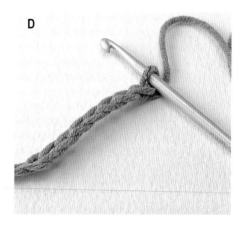

D

Once the foundation chain is complete, you can begin the real work.

DOUBLE CROCHET

A double crochet stitch is one of the most common and frequently used stitches, both for simple and complicated stitch patterns.

1. To make a double crochet stitch, start by wrapping the yarn around the hook in the same way as for making a chain. Insert the hook into the work – the pattern will tell you exactly where this should be – and wrap the yarn over the hook again (**E**).

E

2. Draw through the new loop. Wrap the yarn around the hook again and draw this loop through the last two loops, leaving just two loops on the hook – the new loop and the original loop (**F**).

F

3. Wrap the yarn over the hook again and pull this loop through the two remaining loops on the hook. The new double crochet stitch (**abbreviated to "dc"**) is now completed (**G**).

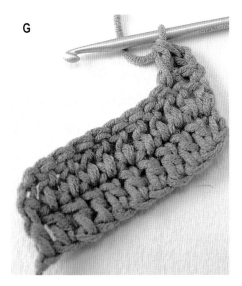

G

POSITIONING THE STITCHES

One of the most important points to remember when following a crochet pattern is to work the new stitches into the correct place. The pattern will tell you exactly where this should be – into a stitch of a previous row or round, into a chain space or into a particular point within the work.

1. Unless a pattern specifies otherwise, when working a new stitch into a previous stitch, insert the hook from the front under both the loops of the "V" of the chain at the top of the stitch (**H**).

H

The only variation to this rule is when working into a chain. Each chain stitch consists of the two bars of yarn that form the "V" and a third bar that sits under them. Work into a chain stitch by inserting the hook into the center of the "V" and under the third bar.

WORKING IN ROWS

Once you have mastered the first few stitches, you are ready to start to put them together to form a crochet fabric. The simplest way to do this is to work them in rows, with the stitches of each row sitting on top of those of the previous row.

While you are working crochet stitches, the hook, and therefore the working loop, are always at the top of the stitch. Crochet stitches are of varying heights, so at the beginning of a new row of crochet you will need to work a few chains to bring the hook up to right height. These chains are know as the "turning chain" and are usually placed at the beginning of the instructions for the row. For example, the pattern will tell you what the turning chain stitches are equal to – 3 ch to replace 1 dc, 1 ch to replace a single crochet, 2 ch to replace a half double crochet, and so on. (See the chart on page 15.)

1. Once the turning chain has been worked, the actual stitches of the row can be started. Remember that the turning chain sits on the last stitch of the previous row, directly below the first stitch of the new row. So, where you have worked a turning chain of 3 ch (to count as the first double crochet of the new row), the next stitch you work will be the second stitch of the row. Count away from the hook until you come to the "V" at the top of the next stitch. The first three "V"s are the turning chain, the next "V" is the last stitch of the previous row. The new stitch must, therefore, be worked into the next stitch to avoid accidentally increasing or decreasing stitches (**I**).

I

2. At the end of a row, remember to work the last stitch of the row into the top of the turning chain at the beginning of the previous row. Otherwise, you risk accidentally increasing or decreasing stitches (**J**).

J

More Stitches

Crochet consists of surprisingly few stitches – it is the way you combine the stitches that creates the patterns. The basic crochet stitches vary in height, from the smallest slip stitch to double trebles, triple trebles, and so on.

SLIP STITCH

This is the smallest of all stitches because it adds no height to the work and is usually used to join two pieces or to move the hook to a new starting point.

1. To make a slip stitch (**abbreviated to "ss"**), insert the hook into the specified place. Wrap the yarn over the hook in the usual way and draw this loop through the stitch the hook was inserted into and the working loop (**A**). This completes the slip stitch.

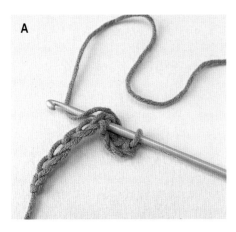

SINGLE CROCHET

This is a slightly taller stitch, standing about one third the height of a double crochet. Frequently used for edgings, this is one of the most well-known crochet stitches.

1. To make a single crochet (**abbreviated to "sc"**), insert the hook into the required point. Wrap the yarn over the hook and draw a loop through the stitch. There are now two loops on the hook.
2. Wrap the yarn around the hook again (**B**) and draw this new loop through both loops on the hook to complete the single crochet.
   When working in single crochet, you will

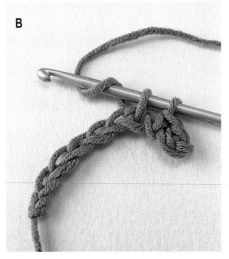

generally find that one chain is added at the beginning of rows, or rounds, as the turning chain. However, sometimes this does NOT count as the first stitch of the new row, or round, but is simply there to raise the hook to the correct point. Make sure you read the pattern correctly to know exactly where the first stitch should be worked.

HALF DOUBLE CROCHET

This stitch is half a double crochet and is about half the height of a double crochet.

1. To make a half double crochet (**abbreviated to "hdc"**), start by making the first half of a double crochet – wrap the yarn over the hook and insert it into the work as detailed in the pattern. Wrap the yarn over the hook again and draw a loop through the stitch. So far, this is like making a double crochet.
2. There are now three loops on the hook. Wrap the yarn over the hook again and draw this new loop through all three loops on the hook to complete the half double crochet (**C**).

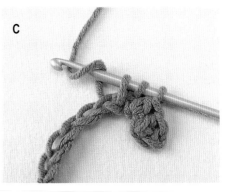

A turning chain of two chains is sufficient to replace a half double crochet.

TREBLE

This stitch is taller than a double crochet. It creates a more open fabric.

1. For a treble (**abbreviated to "tr"**), wrap the yarn around the hook twice before inserting it into the work (**D**). For a double crochet, you would only have wrapped it once.

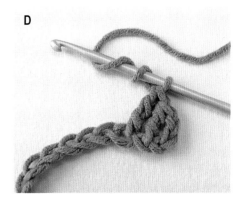

2. Wrap the yarn around the hook again and draw a loop through the work. There are now four loops on the hook. Wrap the yarn around the hook once more and draw this new loop through just the first two loops on the hook, leaving three loops on the hook (**E**).

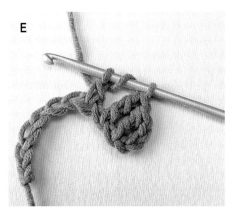

E

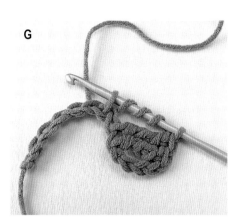

G

3. Again, wrap the yarn over the hook and draw this new loop through just the first two loops on the hook, leaving two loops on the hook. Wrap the yarn over the hook once more (**F**) and draw this loop through the remaining two loops on the hook to complete the treble.

You will normally find a turning chain of four chains used to replace a treble.

2. Now wrap the yarn over the hook and draw this loop through just the first two loops on the hook, leaving four loops on the hook. Repeat this process of wrapping the draw over the hook and drawing the new loop through just the first two loops on the hook until there is just the one new loop remaining on the hook (**H**). The turning chain used to replace a double treble is usually five chains.

as many times as necessary to leave just one loop on the hook.

For a triple treble (**abbreviated to "ttr"**) wrap the yarn round the hook four times. For a quadruple treble (**abbreviated to "qtr"** or **"quad"**) the yarn is wrapped around the hook five times.

When the yarn is wrapped around the hook six times it creates a quintuple treble (**abbreviated to "qtr"** or **"quin tr"**). Note that the abbreviation used for both the quadruple and the quintuple treble is often given as "qtr". This often happens when only one of these two bigger stitches appears in a pattern. Take time to check the abbreviations with a pattern to make sure you are working a stitch of the correct height. It is quite easy to continue making bigger and bigger stitches but they are not used often.

The turning chain needed for these tall stitches depends upon how many times the yarn is wrapped around the hook. Use the guide below for how many turning chains are needed for the various stitches.

STITCH	ABBREVIATION	TURNING CHAIN
single crochet	sc	1 ch
half double crochet	hdc	2 ch
double crochet	dc	3 ch
treble	tr	4 ch
double treble	dtr	5 ch
triple treble	ttr	6 ch
quadruple treble	qtr or quad tr	7 ch
quintuple treble	qtr or quin tr	8 ch

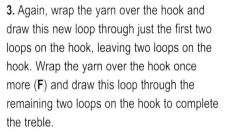

F

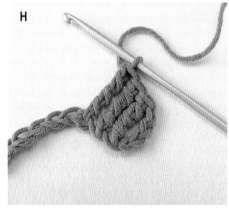

H

DOUBLE TREBLE

This stitch is even taller than the stitches already mentioned. In the same way that a treble has a double wrap of yarn round the hook before being inserted into the work, a double treble has a triple wrapping.

1. Start to make a double treble (**abbreviated to "dtr"**) by wrapping the yarn around the hook three times. Insert the hook into the work, wrap the yarn over the hook again and draw this new loop through the work. This forms five loops on the hook (**G**).

TRIPLE TREBLES AND BIGGER

It is easy to create taller stitches in the same way as for the treble and double treble by increasing the number of times the yarn is wrapped around the hook before it is inserted into the work. No matter how many times the yarn is wrapped around the hook, the way the stitch is worked will not vary. The yarn is wrapped around the hook the number of times needed for this height of stitch. The hook is then inserted into the work, the yarn wrapped around the hook again, and then this new loop drawn through. The process of "yo, draw through 2 loops" is then repeated

FASTENING OFF

When any piece of crochet is complete, you will need to fasten off the work. When the last stitch has been made, cut the yarn leaving a short end of about 2 inches. Wrap this end over the hook and draw this loop through the last stitch, continuing to pull the loop until the cut end comes through as well. You can then very gently pull on this yarn end to tighten the last stitch.

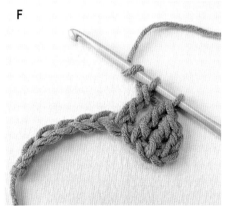

Crochet Diagrams

Crochet is a very visual craft, and the key to its success is the correct placement of each stitch in relation to the rest. And, as a visual craft, it is often easier to understand exactly what you are supposed to do by looking at a visual reference – or crochet diagram – that clearly shows where each stitch sits.

While written crochet patterns are easy to follow for simple textured designs, they can become rather long and wordy when the design is complex, such as for a lacy pattern. In these cases, it is often easier to work the design following a crochet stitch diagram.

These diagrams are basically flat plans of what stitches are worked, in what order, and where they are placed in relation to the other stitches and rows. On the diagram, a different symbol is used to replace each type of stitch and the completed diagram will look similar to the finished work because each symbol will reflect the size of the finished stitch. A tall symbol will be used for a tall stitch and a short symbol for a short stitch.

Accompanying each stitch diagram there should be a key, detailing what each symbol on the chart means. There are standard symbols used for each type of stitch and those used for the basic stitches are listed below:

o	chain (ch)
●	slip stitch (ss)
✕	single crochet (sc)
	half double crochet (hdc)
	double crochet (dc)
	treble (tr)
	double treble (dtr)
	triple treble (ttr)
	quintuple treble (qtr)

The base of each symbol will sit over the stitch into which it is to be worked. Normally the new stitch will be worked into the top of the stitch below, and if this is not the case, the symbol for this new stitch will usually be a variation of the symbol for the "standard" version of the stitch. Take time to look at the key that accompanies the chart to make sure you know what every symbol means, remembering also to refer to the abbreviations until you become comfortable with all of the stitches and abbreviations.

On the stitch diagram, you will also find various symbols to provide other pieces of information you will need to know, such as:

◀	start here
◁	fasten off here
⟶	direction of work

Apart from these symbols, you will also find numbers that relate to the row or round being worked. They usually appear at the beginning of that row or round.

If you choose to follow a stitch diagram, it is best to start by working the foundation chain and the first one or two rows or rounds following the written instructions. This will give you an idea of what shape you are working. Once this little section is complete, it is usually quite simple to switch over and follow the stitch diagram for the following rows or rounds. But remember to refer back to the instructions from time to time to make sure you have the correct number of stitches and to know when to do any shaping.

Sometimes a section of the work will be repeated more than once, which is known as the "stitch repeat." On most crochet stitch diagrams, the section that needs to be repeated to complete each row or round will be indicated either by a pair of dashed lines or a pair of asterisks. On a circular design, often the whole of the first few rounds will be shown, and after that point only one or two of the stitch repeats, creating a wedge-shaped diagram. Simply follow this "wedge" section, working it repeatedly around the central-base section to complete the circle. It is usually obvious how many times you need to repeat the wedge, but if you are unsure, it is best to refer to the instructions for details.

For simple textured designs with a stitch repeat of one or two stitches, or sometimes up to 4 or 5 stitches, the stitch diagram may not tell you how many times to work the repeat to fill the row. This should be obvious from the size of the work. Again, if in any doubt, refer to the instructions.

Whether you follow the instructions or the stitch diagram, you should achieve the same results. And often a combination of the two is the best option.

A SIMPLE DOUBLE CROCHET FABRIC

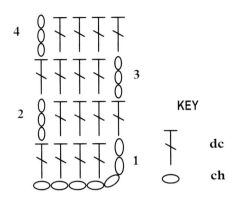

KEY

dc

ch

ABOVE: This stitch diagram shows a simple double crochet fabric. Here the "stitch repeat" is just one stitch. One double crochet is worked into each double crochet of the previous row, and so no stitch repeat is marked on the diagram. Each stitch sits above the previous row and the turning chains are worked and used at each end of the rows.

A TWO-STITCH REPEAT

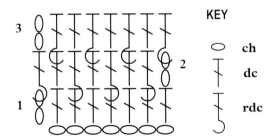

KEY

ch

dc

rdc

ABOVE: This stitch diagram, as used for the blankets on page 68, is another simple textured stitch repeat. Here there is just a two-stitch repeat, which is not marked on the diagram, but it is not necessary. The stitches used to create this fabric are relief double crochet stitches. Refer to the diagram and key, and you will see that the symbol used for each relief double crochet is a variation of the symbol used for a standard double crochet. It has a little hook on the bottom showing that the stitch is worked in a different way than other double crochets.

A THREE-STITCH REPEAT

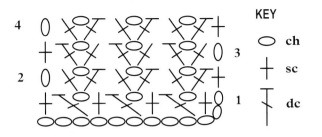

KEY

ch

sc

dc

ABOVE: A stitch diagram for a simple three-stitch repeat, used for the crochet bags on page 28, does not have a stitch repeat marked on it and only shows a total of 11 stitches, even though the actual work is much wider. It illustrates how to work the beginning and end of every row, and how each group of three new stitches sits above those of the previous row.

A MOTIF STITCH DIAGRAM

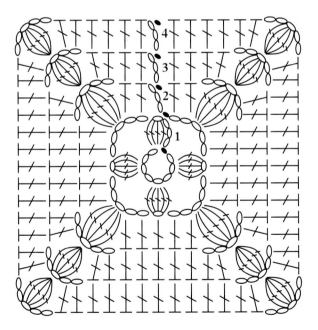

ABOVE: A stitch diagram for a motif such as this one, used for the bedspread on page 49, may show the first few rounds. By the time these rounds have been completed it should be quite simple to see exactly how each future round is added to complete the full motif.

KEY

dc

ch

ss

popcorn

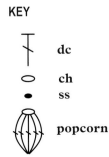

Patchwork Throw

Mix natural tones and textures to make this color block patchwork throw. It's made in strips using the simplest of stitches.

MEASUREMENTS

Finished throw is approx 51 inches wide and 59 inches long.

MATERIALS

Rowan All Seasons Cotton (1¾ oz. per ball): 4 balls in first color (A – pale beige)

Rowan Chunky Cotton Chenille (3½ oz. per ball): 3 balls in second color (B – beige) and 3 balls in fourth color (D – cream)

Rowan Kid Classic (1¾ oz. per ball): 4 balls in third color (C – cream)

Rowan Magpie Aran (3½ oz. per hank): 2 hanks in fifth color (E – cream marl), and 2 hanks in sixth color (F – cream)

Rowan Rowanspun Aran (3½ oz. per hank): 3 hanks in seventh color (G – cream)

Size H crochet hook

GAUGE

14 sts and 7½ rows to 4 inches measured over double crochet fabric using a size H hook, or size required to give correct gauge.

ABBREVIATIONS

See page 11.

THROW

The throw is worked in 6 striped strips that will be sewn together. When working strips, use two strands of Rowan Kid Classic held together and one strand of all other yarns.

First Strip

Using size H hook and A, make 34 ch.
Foundation row: 1 dc into 4th ch from hook, 1 dc into each ch to end, turn. 32 sts.
Now, work in double crochet fabric as follows:

Row 1: 3 ch (counts as 1 dc), skip dc at base of 3 ch, 1 dc into each dc to end, working last dc into top of turning ch, turn.
This row forms double crochet fabric.
Continue even until Strip measures 8 inches.
Break off yarn A and join in yarn C.
Cont even until Strip measures 12½ inches.
Break off yarn C and join in yarn D.
Cont even until Strip measures 24½ inches.
Break off yarn D and join in yarn F.
Cont even until Strip measures 35½ inches.
Break off yarn F and join in yarn B.
Cont even until Strip measures 42½ inches.
Break off yarn B and join in yarn C.
Cont even until Strip measures 49½ inches.
Break off yarn C and join in yarn D.
Cont even until Strip measures 52 inches.
Break off yarn D and join in yarn E.
Cont even until Strip measures 59 inches.
Fasten off.

Second Strip

Using a size H hook and G, make 13 ch.
Work foundation row as for First Strip. 11 sts.
Now work in double crochet fabric as for First Strip as follows:
Cont even until Strip measures 11 inches.
Break off yarn G and join in yarn E.
Cont even until Strip measures 19½ inches.
Break off yarn E and join in yarn A.
Cont even until Strip measures 21¼ inches.

KEY

$\dagger$ dc

$\bigcirc$ ch

ABOVE: This diagram shows the double crochet fabric used to make the strips for the throw. At the start of every row, there are three turning chains, that replace the first double crochet. The last double crochet of every row is worked into the top of the turning chain at the beginning of the previous row. A double crochet fabric such as this does not really have a stitch repeat because one double crochet is worked into the top of each double crochet of the previous row.

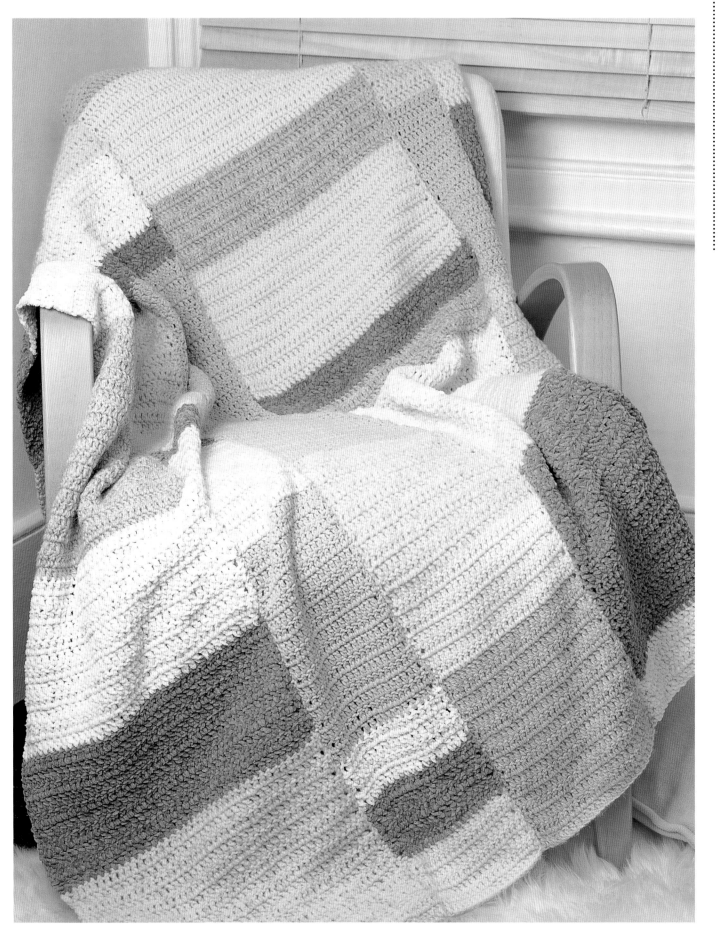

Break off yarn A and join in yarn G.
Cont even until Strip measures
33 inches.
Break off yarn G and join in yarn A.
Cont even until Strip measures
45 inches.
Break off yarn A and join in yarn G.
Cont even until Strip measures
51 inches.
Break off yarn G and join in yarn B.
Cont even until Strip measures
59 inches.
Fasten off.

Third Strip

Using size H hook and D, make 51 ch.
Work foundation row as for First Strip.
49 sts.
Now work in double crochet fabric as for
First Strip as follows:
Cont even until Strip measures 3 inches.
Break off yarn D and join in yarn B.
Cont even until Strip measures
15¾ inches.
Break off yarn B and join in yarn C.
Cont even until Strip measures
18 inches.
Break off yarn C and join in yarn F.
Cont even until Strip measures
23 inches.
Break off yarn F and join in yarn D.
Cont even until Strip measures
31½ inches.
Break off yarn D and join in yarn E.
Cont even until Strip measures
34 inches.
Break off yarn E and join in yarn B.
Cont even until Strip measures
36¼ inches.
Break off yarn B and join in yarn C.
Cont even until Strip measures
43½ inches.
Break off yarn C and join in yarn E.
Cont even until Strip measures
48 inches.
Break off yarn E and join in yarn F.
Cont even until Strip measures
54½ inches.
Break off yarn F and join in yarn A.

Cont even until Strip measures
59 inches
Fasten off.

Fourth Strip

Using size H hook and E, make 30 ch.
Work foundation row as for First Strip.
28 sts.
Now work in double crochet fabric as for
First Strip as follows:
Cont even until Strip measures
9½ inches.
Break off yarn E and join in yarn F.
Cont even until Strip measures
13½ inches.
Break off yarn F and join in yarn G.
Cont even until Strip measures
22 inches.
Break off yarn G and join in yarn A.
Cont even until Strip measures
44 inches.
Break off yarn A and join in yarn B.
Cont even until Strip measures
45½ inches.
Break off yarn B and join in yarn D.
Cont even until Strip measures
49½ inches.
Break off yarn D and join in yarn C.

ABOVE: Crocheted seams (see page 25), on the wrong side of the throw, have a neat appearance.

Cont even until Strip measures 59 inches. Fasten off.

Fifth Strip

Using size H hook and C, make 22 ch.
Work foundation row as for First Strip.
20 sts.
Now work in double crochet fabric as for First Strip as follows:
Cont until Strip measures 4 inches.
Break off yarn C and join in yarn B.
Cont even until Strip measures 6¼ inches.
Break off yarn B and join in yarn D.
Cont even until Strip measures 8½ inches.
Break off yarn D and join in yarn A.
Cont even until Strip measures 19 inches.
Break off yarn A and join in yarn F.
Cont even until Strip measures 25 inches.
Break off yarn F and join in yarn B.
Cont even until Strip measures 27½ inches.
Break off yarn B and join in yarn C.
Cont until Strip measures 33 inches.

Break off yarn C and join in yarn G.
Cont even until Strip measures 59 inches.
Fasten off.

Sixth Strip

Using size H hook and G, make 44 ch.
Work foundation row as for First Strip.
42 sts.
Now work in double crochet fabric as for First Strip as follows:
Cont even until Strip measures 11 inches.
Break off yarn G and join in yarn B.
Cont even until Strip measures 16½ inches.
Break off yarn B and join in yarn D.
Cont even until Strip measures 23½ inches.
Break off yarn D and join in yarn E.
Cont even until Strip measures 36¼ inches.
Break off yarn E and join in yarn F.
Cont even until Strip measures 37¾ inches.
Break off yarn F and join in yarn D.
Cont even until Strip measures 42¼ inches.
Break off yarn D and join in yarn B.
Cont even until Strip measures 47¼ inches.
Break off yarn B and join in yarn A.
Cont even until Strip measures 55 inches.
Break off yarn A and join in yarn F.
Cont even until Strip measures 59 inches. Fasten off.

Finishing

Matching foundation chain edges, attach the First Strip to the Second, the Second to the Third and so on. Use a large-eyed needle and one of the smooth yarns used in the throw and oversew the edges. If you wish to use crocheted seams, see page 25. Make sure the strips lay smoothly next to each other, without any puckering or pulling. Once all the seams are joined, press carefully from the wrong side, covering the work with a cloth (see page 48).

Working in Rounds

One of the great joys of crochet is that it is very easy to create circular pieces because there is only one stitch to work. These circular pieces can either be flat for making a place mat or tablecloth, shaped circles for hats, or tubular pieces that need no seaming afterwards.

Most crochet is worked from right to left. To create a fabric by working in rows, you need to turn the work at the end of each row before beginning the next row.

When working in rounds, there is no need to keep turning the work. However, as you still need to raise the height of the working loop to the required point for the new round, you will still need to work a "turning" chain at the beginning of each round.

JOINING THE ENDS OF A ROUND

1. When you reach the end of a round, join the end of this round to its beginning by working a slip stitch into the top of the turning chain (**A**). Sometimes, to create a particular effect, you will join the round in a different way, but this will be explained in your pattern.

A

2. Begin the new round by working the required number of turning chain. It is called a turning chain whether you turn the work or not. The stitch closing the previous round was worked into the first stitch of the previous row and the turning chain will be standing on this stitch (**B**). So as when working in rows, the first stitch you work when beginning this new round will be the second stitch of the row.

B

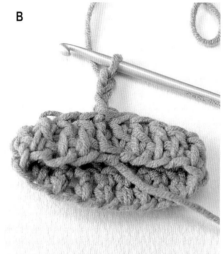

Crochet stitches viewed from the front look different when viewed from the back. A crochet fabric made up of rows of double crochets will have both sides of the double crochet stitches showing – one row revealing the front of the stitches, with the next row showing the backs of the stitches.

When making a fabric from double crochets when the work is not turned before each new round, only one side of all the double crochets will show and the fabric will look

different. To create the same fabric when working in rounds as in rows, it's essential to turn the work at the end of every round.

Sometimes, to create a particular effect, the pattern will require you to turn the work at certain points. Make sure you note whether or not a pattern indicates turning the work at the ends of the rounds.

STARTING A CIRCULAR PIECE

Working in rounds of crochet can form flat circles of crochet to make place mats and tablecloths or three-dimensional tubes and bowl-shapes to make hats or bags.

Whatever shape you are making, you will generally start with a foundation chain.

1. Make the foundation chain as detailed in the pattern and then join the two ends by working a slip stitch into the first chain stitch. Be sure the chain is not twisted before you join the ends. (**C**)

C

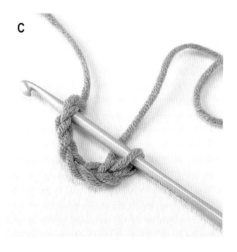

2. Where you have worked a fairly long foundation chain, you will work the first round into the chain stitches in the usual way.

However, if the foundation chain was very short, you will have a small ring of chain, rather than a large loop, once the ends are joined. Here the stitches of the first round will often be worked into the center of this ring (**D**), rather than into each individual stitch, enclosing the whole of the chain. This is often the case when starting a hat at the crown point or a motif or place mat at the center.

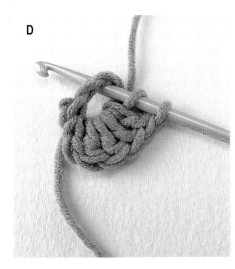

D

You will find that there are normally two to three times as many stitches worked into the ring as there are chain stitches making up the ring. This tends to fill in the ring and, more often than not, there is virtually no hole left at the center.

CLOSING THE CENTER HOLE

Sometimes a design will require that there be absolutely no hole left at the center. In these cases a slip loop is made to replace the foundation chain, and the stitches of the first round are worked into this slip loop.

1. Make a slip loop around the hook but do not tighten it (**E**). Note that this loop is NOT the same as the usual starting slip knot shown on page 12.

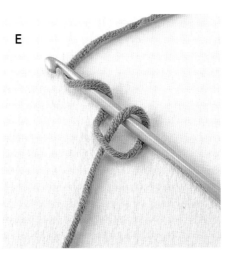

E

2. Now, working into the center of this loose loop, work the required stitches – when working into a slip loop, these are normally short single crochet stitches (**F**).

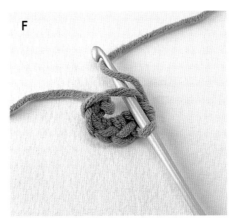

F

3. Once the round is completed, join the ends of the round with a slip stitch. Now gently pull on the loose yarn end to tighten the slip loop and to close the center hole (**G**).

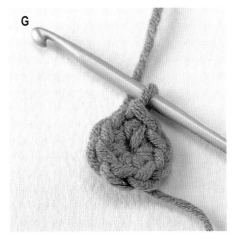

G

FASTENING OFF

When any piece of crochet is complete, you will need to fasten off the work. When the last stitch has been made, cut the yarn leaving a short end of about 2 inches. Wrap this end over the hook in the normal way and draw this loop through the last stitch, continuing to pull the loop until the cut end comes through as well. You can then very gently pull on this yarn end to tighten the last stitch.

1. When working in rounds, fasten off once the ends of the last round have been joined. Whether working in rows or rounds, if the pieces are to be joined afterwards to make the final item, it is sometimes a good idea to leave a fairly long end when fastening off. This end can then be used to sew any seams, avoiding the need to join in new lengths of yarn and reducing the number of loose ends that need to be darned in (**H**).

H

Decreasing Stitches

When shaping a piece of crochet, there will be times when you will have to reduce the number of stitches. The way this is achieved depends on the number of stitches to be lost and where along a row or round to lose them.

DECREASING AT THE END OF A ROW

1. To reduce several stitches at the end of a row, simply end the row earlier by the required number of stitches. For example, to decrease three stitches at the end of the row, work across the row until there are just three stitches left – remember the turning chain at the beginning of the previous row will count as one of these stitches (**A**). Now turn the work and start the next row by working the turning chain. This turning chain will sit on the new row end stitch.

DECREASING AT THE BEGINNING OF A ROW

1. To reduce stitches at the beginning of a row, work slip stitches into each stitch that needs to be decreased and begin the row in the next stitch. For example, to decrease three stitches at the beginning of a row, start this row by working a slip stitch into each of the first three stitches. Now work a slip stitch into the next stitch – the new "first" stitch – and then work the required turning chain before completing the new, shorter row (**B**).

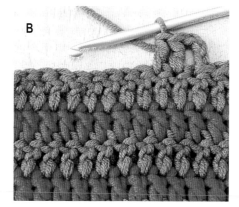

WORKING TWO STITCHES TOGETHER

There are two ways to decrease a stitch within a row or round. The simplest way is to skip a stitch – but this can leave a hole in the work that can spoil the finished look. The better option is to work two stitches together.

1. To work two double crochet stitches together, start by making the first double crochet up to the last "yo and draw through last 2 loops on hook" point that would complete the stitch. Now work the next double crochet up to exactly the same point. There are now three loops on the hook (**C**).

2. Wrap the yarn around the hook and draw this loop through, thereby completing both double crochets at the same time (**D**).

It is possible to decrease in this way when working most stitches – even short, single crochet stitches. Work each stitch up to the last stage, and then complete both stitches at the same time.

This method can also be used to decrease more than one stitch – depending on the height of the stitch, up to three or four stitches can be worked together in this way.

This type of decrease has its own abbreviation and this abbreviation will vary depending on the type and number of stitches being used. Working two single crochet together to decrease one stitch will be abbreviated to **"sc2tog,"** while working three double crochets together to decrease two stitches is abbreviated as **"dc3tog."**

Joining Seams

Crochet projects are often made up of more than one piece that need to be joined together neatly to create the final item. There are a variety of ways in which pieces can be seamed together.

Because of the nature of crochet fabrics, it will be virtually impossible to create an invisible seam, but the joins can be neat and even. It is best to press the crochet pieces before joining them and to then press just the seams once they have been sewn.

SEWING SEAMS

Crochet pieces can be joined by hand sewing them together. Use the same yarn for the seams as used to crochet the item and a blunt-pointed needle with an eye large enough to thread with this yarn. Needles designed for sewing up hand knits or for tapestry are ideal.

1. Hold the two crochet sections right sides facing and join the seam by sewing the two edges together, taking in just one strand of yarn along each edge. Place the stitches close together so that the two layers are held together securely. Depending on the amount taken into the seam and the type of crochet stitch, this seam may lie totally flat – or form a slight ridge on the inside (**A**).

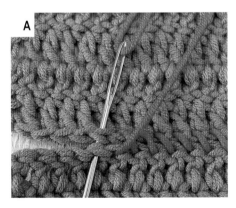

If a perfectly flat seam is required, join the two edges by butting them up against each other. Using the needle and yarn, work a stitch into one edge and then the other, gently pulling the two edges together as you go along. If worked correctly, the stitching should be invisible and the two edges should sit tightly next to each other. This is not, however, a very flexible seam and is probably best avoided when sewing garment seams.

CROCHETING SEAMS

The most flexible way of joining two pieces of crochet is to work a line of crochet along the edges, working through both edges.

1. Hold the two pieces to be joined right sides facing. Join the two pieces by working a line of single crochet along the edge, inserting the hook through both layers of crochet for each single crochet stitch. Place the stitches close to each other, and try to take an even amount into the seam. Just one strand of yarn from each edge should be sufficient (**B**).

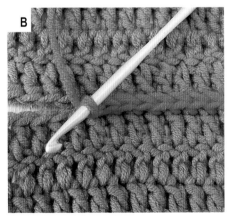

The crochet seam can be worked as a line of slip stitching if preferred. However, whatever stitch is used for the seam, there will be a definite ridge along the seam line on the inside.

JOINING MOTIFS

Depending on the type of motif you are making, you can either join them together once completed, or join as you work the last part of the motif.

1. If the motifs are to be joined as they are made, the pattern will give you details of how this is to be done. Motifs are often held wrong sides together when being joined (**C**).

2. If the motifs are to be joined afterwards, it is best done by crocheting them together. Hold two motifs together and work the crochet along the edges to join them, working one seam stitch for every stitch along the edge of the motif. This seam creates a definite ridge that is sometimes used as a decorative detail. Check the pattern to find out whether this seam is to sit on the right or wrong side of the work (**D**).

Joining in New Yarn and Colors

Most crochet items will use more than one ball of yarn and many use more than one color. One of the beauties of crochet is how easy it is to add multiple colors. But work neatly to avoid spoiling the look of the work.

When working in rows, always try to join in new balls of yarn at the end of a row – any long ends left along the side of the work can be used to join the seams later. If this is not possible, or when working in the round, choose a point to join in the new yarn where you feel it will be both least visible and easiest to join.

1. To join in new yarn or a different color at any point, work the last stitch using the old ball, or color, up to the point where the last "yo and draw this loop through to complete the stitch" is reached. Now let this yarn fall at the back of the work and pick up the new yarn, or color. Complete the stitch with this new ball of yarn, leaving two yarn ends at the back of the work (**A**). Once the crochet is completed, the yarn ends can be neatly darned in to the back of the work.

2. Depending on the type of stitch pattern being worked, it is possible to enclose the ends of the yarn inside the following stitches. Simply let them sit on top of the previous row, between the "V"s of the stitches, and work the next five or six stitches enclosing these ends as well (**B**). Leave the ends free at the back of the work beyond this point and, afterwards, gently pull on the yarn ends and trim away the excess.

When joining in yarn to work a new section such as an edging, first make a slip loop around the hook. Now work a slip stitch into the crochet work at the point where the yarn needs to be joined in. You are then ready to start the row or round.

Increasing Stitches

If you are making a shaped piece of crochet, you will have to work decreases and add extra stitches as well. The way this is done will depend upon where the increased stitches must fall within the work.

Not every crochet section will be just a tube or rectangle. Sometimes you will need to shape the work by increasing its width and the number of stitches in each row or round. Depending upon the effect to be achieved, there are many ways this can be done.

TO INCREASE ONE STITCH AT ANY POINT

1. To increase one stitch at any point within a row, or round, work two stitches into the same point on the previous row or round (**A**).

If you need to increase by more than one stitch, this can be done in the same way. Simply work the required number of stitches into the same place. Keep in mind that too many stitches worked into one place can distort the work. If you need to increase by more than three stitches, it is best to evenly spread out the increased stitches over the whole row or round, working two stitches into one at evenly spaced intervals.

Working several stitches into a particular point is also used to create fancy stitch patterns. Lots of stitches are worked into one

base stitch and then the same number of stitches are skipped when working on along the row or round, thereby keeping the final number of stitches the same. (See page 40.) Before you work any "increases" of this sort, check that the pattern means to increase stitches, rather than just create an effect.

TO INCREASE SEVERAL STITCHES AT THE BEGINNING OF A ROW

1. To increase at the beginning of a row, you will need to make a foundation chain for these new stitches. Before beginning the row, work a chain for each new stitch needed and then work the required turning chain for the type of stitch you are using. Then work the new stitches as needed, continuing on across the previous row (**B**).

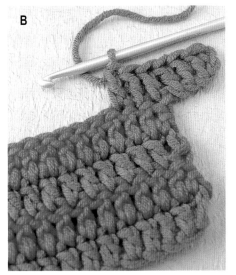

For example, to increase three double crochets at the beginning of a row, make three chains (one for each new stitch) and then two more chains. These last three chain form the first stitch, so the second new (double cro-

chet) stitch will be worked into the fourth chain counting away from the hook. The third increased stitch will be worked into the next chain and the following stitch will be worked into the last stitch of the previous row.

TO INCREASE SEVERAL STITCHES AT THE END OF A ROW

1. To increase several stitches at the end of a row, make a new separate foundation chain for these stitches. For example, to increase five stitches at the end of a row, make a foundation chain of five chains using an oddment of the main yarn. Work across the row to the end of the row until the stitch has been worked into the top of the turning chain at the beginning of the previous row. Now work stitches into each of the new foundation chain stitches before turning the work (**C**).

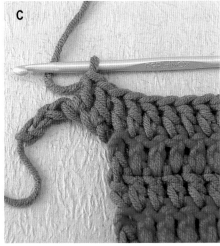

When working a complex stitch pattern, or a lacy design, you will generally find that the row, or round, instructions will be written to include any necessary increases so that the pattern will follow through correctly.

Shopping Bags

You can shop till you drop and not worry about carrying it all home when you make these useful shoulder bags.

MEASUREMENTS

Shopper is approx 12½ inches wide and 12 inches tall.
Shoulder bag is approx 6¼ inches wide and 7¾ inches tall.

MATERIALS

For the Shopper:
Wendy Supreme Luxury Cotton DK (3½ oz. per ball): 3 balls in Main Color (M - beige) and 1 ball of same yarn in Contrast Color (C - white)

For the Shoulder bag:
Rowan Denim (1¾ oz. per ball): 3 balls
1 button

For either bag:
Size D and size E crochet hooks

GAUGE

Shopper: 25 sts and 15 rows measured over the textured pattern, 20 sts and 14 rows measured over the half double crochet fabric to 4 inches using a size E hook, or size required to give correct gauge.

Shoulder bag: Before washing, 21 sts and 13 rows, after washing 25 sts and 15 rows measured over the textured pattern, 20 sts and 14 rows measured over the half double crochet fabric to 4 inches using a size E hook, or size required to give correct gauge.

Note: Rowan Denim yarn shrinks when washed. Allowances have been made in the Shoulder Bag pattern for this shrinkage.

KEY

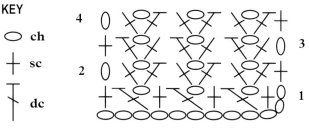

ABBREVIATIONS

hdc2tog = (yo and insert hook as indicated, yo and draw loop through) twice, yo and draw through all 5 loops on hook.
See also page 11.

BAGS

SIDES (Make 2)

Using a size E hook and M, make 81 ch.

Row 1: (1 sc, 1 ch and 1 dc) into 3rd ch from hook, skip 2 ch, *(1 sc, 1 ch and 1 dc) into next ch, skip 2 ch, rep from * to last ch, 1 sc into last ch, turn. 26 patt repeats, 80 sts.

Row 2: 1 ch (counts as first st), skip (1 sc and 1 dc) at end of last row, *(1 sc, 1 ch and 1 dc) into next ch sp★★, skip (1 sc and 1 dc), rep from * to end, ending last rep at ★★, 1 sc into top of turning ch, turn.

Row 2 forms textured patt.

Cont in textured patt until work measures 7 inches.

Join in C and work 2 rows.

Using M work a further 6 rows.

Using C, work another 2 rows.

ABOVE: This stitch diagram shows the stitch pattern used for the lower section of both bags. Each row of the pattern consists of groups of a single crochet, chain and double crochet that sit on top of the matching group of the previous row. At the beginning of each row, work one chain to bring the new row up to the required height, and complete the row by working a single crochet into the chain at the beginning of the previous row. Between these two stitches, repeat the groups of three stitches as many times as required.

NOTE:
Pattern is written for the Shopper, followed by the Shoulder Bag (shown right) in bold in square brackets. Where only one set of figures is given, this refers to both bags. For the Shoulder Bag, ignore references to M and C and use same color throughout.

LEFT: The Shopper is the larger of the two bags and has two bold stripes in a contrasting color.

Break off C and cont using M only.

Cont even until work measures 10½ [7¾] inches.

Change to size D hook.

Next row: 2 ch (counts as first st), *1 hdc into each of next 2 sts, hdc2tog over next 2 sts**, 1 hdc into next st, rep from * to end, ending last rep at ** and working last hdc into top of turning ch, turn. 64 sts.

Next row: 2 ch (counts as first hdc), 1 hdc into each hdc to end, working last hdc into top of turning ch, turn.

Rep last row until work measures 12½ [9½] inches.

Fasten off.

Shape first strap

Skip first 6 [8] sts of next row, rejoin yarn to next st with a ss and cont as follows:-

★★Row 1: 2 ch, skip st at base of 2 ch, 1 hdc

Shape second strap

Return to last complete row worked, skip 20 [16] sts after first strap, rejoin yarn to next st with a ss and work second strap to match first from ★★ to ★★.

Holding straps with RS tog and taking care not to twist straps, join ends of straps by working a row of sc through sts of both straps.

Fasten off.

Finishing

Shopper only: Join Sides together along side edges and base. Using size D hook and M, work one round of sc evenly around edges of straps and upper edge, ending with ss to first sc. Press.

Shoulder bag only: Fold bag in half to form a tube and join row ends to form back seam.

into each of next 15 sts, turn. 16 sts.

Row 2: 2 ch (counts as first st), hdc2tog over next 2 sts, 1 hdc into each st to last 3 sts, hdc2tog over next 2 sts, 1 hdc into top of turning ch, turn.

Rep row 2, 5 times more. 4 sts.

Row 8: 2 ch (counts as first st), 1 hdc into each st to end, working last hdc into top of turning ch, turn.

Rep row 8 only until strap measures 13¾ [27½] inches.

Fasten off.★★

Re-fold bag so that seam runs centrally down back between folds and sew base seam.

Using size D hook, work one round of sc evenly around edges of strap and upper edge, ending with ss to first sc and working button loop midway across front edge of bag as follows: 9 ch, turn, 1 sc into 5th ch from hook, 1 sc into each of next 4 ch. Sew on button to correspond with button loop.

Machine wash bag on a hot setting to shrink bag to correct size. Press.

Dressing-Table Set

Adorn your dressing table with these little lacy doilies. The larger doily is made by simply crocheting seven of the smaller ones and joining them together. Try joining more motifs, honeycomb style, to create a doily or cloth of any size.

MEASUREMENTS

Finished small mat is 4¼ inches in diameter.
Finished large mat is 10½ inches in diameter.

MATERIALS

Anchor Pearl Cotton No. 8 (¼ oz. per ball): 2 balls in white
Size B crochet hook

GAUGE

First 3 rounds measures 1¾ inches in diameter using size B hook, or size required to give correct gauge.

ABBREVIATIONS

dc4tog = *yo and insert hook as indicated, yo and draw loop through, yo and draw through 2 loops, rep from * 3 times more, yo and draw through all 5 loops on hook.
dc5tog = *yo and insert hook as indicated, yo and draw loop through, yo and draw through 2 loops, rep from * 4 times more, yo and draw through all 6 loops on hook.
See also page 11.

SMALL DOILY

Using size B hook, make 6 ch and join with a ss to form a ring.

Round 1: 1 ch, 12 sc into ring, ss to first sc.

Round 2: 1 ch, 1 sc into st at base of 1 ch, [7 ch, skip 1 sc, 1 sc into next sc] 5 times, 3 ch, 1 tr into top of sc at beg of round.

Round 3: 3 ch, 4 dc into ch sp formed by tr at end of previous round, [3 ch, 5 dc into next ch sp] 5 times, 3 ch, ss to top of 3 ch at beg of round.

Round 4: 3 ch, skip st at base of 3 ch, 1 dc into each of next 4 dc, *3 ch, 1 sc into next ch sp, 3 ch**, 1 dc into each of next 5 dc, rep from * to end, ending last rep at **, ss to top of 3 ch at beg of round.

Round 5: 3 ch, skip st at base of 3 ch, dc4tog over next 4 dc, *[5 ch, 1 sc into next ch sp] twice**, 5 ch, dc5tog over next 5 dc, rep from * to end, ending last rep at **, 2 ch, 1 dc into top of dc4tog at beg of round.

Round 6: 1 ch, 1 sc into ch sp formed by dc at end of previous round, [5 ch, 1 sc into next ch sp] 17 times, 2 ch, 1 dc into top of sc at beg of round.

Round 7: 1 ch, 1 sc into ch sp formed by dc at end of previous round, *3 ch, (5 dc, 3 ch and 5 dc) into next ch sp, 3 ch, 1 sc into next ch sp, 5 ch**, 1 sc into next ch sp, rep from * to end, ending last rep at **, ss to top of sc at beg of round.

Fasten off.

LARGE DOILY

The large doily is seven of the small ones joined together – one central doily with six more surrounding it. Each one is a hexagon. You can be join them by sewing them together where they meet at the corners and midway along the sides. Alternatively you can join them while you are working the last round. To do it while working round 7, replace the (3 ch) at the corner to be joined with (1 ch, 1 ss into corresponding ch loop

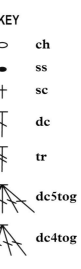

LEFT: This stitch diagram shows the entire design of one of the smaller doilies.

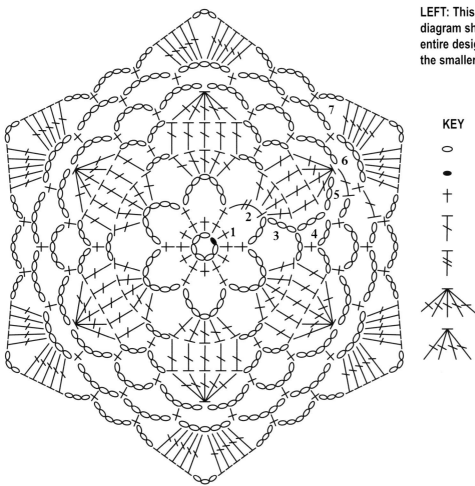

KEY

○	ch
●	ss
+	sc
┼	dc
╪	tr
⋀	dc5tog
⋀	dc4tog

on adjacent hexagon, 1 ch), and replace the (5 ch) at the center of a side with (2 ch, 1 ss into corresponding ch loop on adjacent hexagon, 2 ch). Join hexagons holding them with WS together.

To Finish
Pin out to measurement given, dampen, and leave to dry naturally.

Fun Sun Hats

These delightful sun hats are great for children of all ages. Choose from bright sunny hues for a toddler to subtler colors for older children and adults.

MEASUREMENTS

To fit average size toddler [child,adult] head Width around head is 17¼ [19¼,20¾] inches).

MATERIALS

For a hat in one color: Rowan Handknit DK Cotton (1¾ oz. per ball): 2 [3,3] balls
Size E crochet hook
Toddler's hat used 1 ball in each of four colors – green, orange, yellow and red
Child's hat used 1 ball in each of 3 colors – navy, turquoise and green
Adult's hat used 2 balls in each of 2 colors – dark beige and mid beige

GAUGE

18 sts and 12 rows to 4 inches measured over half double crochet fabric using size E hook, or size required to give correct gauge.

ABBREVIATIONS

See page 11.

ONE-COLOR HAT

Using size E hook, make 4 ch and join with a ss to form a ring.
Round 1: 2 ch (counts as 1 hdc), 7 hdc into ring, ss to top of 2 ch at beg of round. 8 sts.
Round 2: 2 ch (counts as 1 hdc), 1 hdc into st at base of 2 ch, 2 hdc into each of next 7 hdc, ss to top of 2 ch at beg of round. 16 sts.
Round 3: 2 ch (counts as 1 hdc), 1 hdc into st at base of 2 ch, 1 hdc into next hdc, (2 hdc into next hdc, 1 hdc into next hdc) 7 times, ss to top of 2 ch at beg of round. 24 sts.
Round 4: 2 ch (counts as 1 hdc), 1 hdc into st at base of 2 ch, 1 hdc into each of next 2 hdc, (2 hdc into next hdc, 1 hdc into each of next 2 hdc) 7 times, ss to top of 2 ch at beg of round. 32 sts.
Round 5: 2 ch (counts as 1 hdc), 1 hdc into st at base of 2 ch, 1 hdc into each of next 3 hdc, (2 hdc into next hdc, 1 hdc into each of next 3 hdc) 7 times, ss to top of 2 ch at beg of round. 40 sts.
Round 6: 2 ch (counts as 1 hdc), 1 hdc into st at base of 2 ch, 1 hdc into each of next 4 hdc, (2 hdc into next hdc, 1 hdc into each of next 4 hdc) 7 times, ss to top of 2 ch at beg of round. 48 sts.
Round 7: 2 ch (counts as 1 hdc), 1 hdc into st at base of 2 ch, 1 hdc into each of next 5 hdc, (2 hdc into next hdc, 1 hdc into each of next 5 hdc) 7 times, ss to top of 2 ch at beg of round. 56 sts.
Round 8: 2 ch (counts as 1 hdc), 1 hdc into st at base of 2 ch, 1 hdc into each of next 6 hdc, (2 hdc into next hdc, 1 hdc into each of next 6 hdc) 7 times, ss to top of 2 ch at beg of round. 64 sts.
Round 9: 2 ch (counts as 1 hdc), 1 hdc into st at base of 2 ch, 1 hdc into each of next 7 hdc, (2 hdc into next hdc, 1 hdc into each of next 7 hdc) 7 times, ss to top of 2 ch at beg of round. 72 sts.
Round 10: 2 ch (counts as 1 hdc), 1 hdc into st at base of 2 ch, 1 hdc into each of next 8 hdc, (2 hdc into next hdc, 1 hdc into each of next 8 hdc) 7 times, ss to top of 2 ch at beg of round. 80 sts.

Child and adult sizes only

Round 11: 2 ch (counts as 1 hdc), 1 hdc into st at base of 2 ch, 1 hdc into each of next 9 hdc, (2 hdc into next hdc, 1 hdc into each of next 9 hdc) 7 times, ss to top of 2 ch at beg of round. 88 sts.

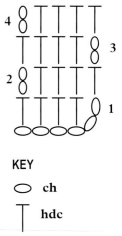

KEY

◯ ch

⊤ hdc

ABOVE: This stitch diagram shows the basic half-double crochet fabric used for the hats. Although this diagram shows the fabric as rows, the turning chains at the beginning of each row will still be worked for each new round. At the end of every round, work a slip stitch into the top of this turning chain to close the round. The turning chain for the new round will sit on top of the turning chain of each previous row.

Adult size only

Round 12: 2 ch (counts as 1 hdc), 1 hdc into st at base of 2 ch, 1 hdc into each of next 10 hdc, (2 hdc into next hdc, 1 hdc into each of next 10 hdc) 7 times, ss to top of 2 ch at beg of round. 96 sts.

All sizes

Next round: 2 ch (counts as 1 hdc), 1 hdc into each hdc to end, ss to top of 2 ch at beg of round.
Rep last round 7 [8,9] times more.

Shape brim

Round 1: 2 ch (counts as 1 hdc), 1 hdc into st at base of 2 ch, 1 hdc into each of next 7 hdc, *2 hdc into next hdc, 1 hdc into each of next 7 hdc, rep from * to end, ss to top of 2 ch at beg of round. 90 [99,108] sts.

Round 2: 2 ch (counts as 1 hdc), 1 hdc into each hdc to end, ss to top of 2 ch at beg of round.

Round 3: 2 ch (counts as 1 hdc), 1 hdc into st at base of 2 ch, 1 hdc into each of next 8 hdc, *2 hdc into next hdc, 1 hdc into each of next 8 hdc, rep from * to end, ss to top of 2 ch at beg of round. 100 [110,120] sts.

Round 4: 2 ch (counts as 1 hdc), 1 hdc into each hdc to end, ss to top of 2 ch at beg of round.

Round 5: 2 ch (counts as 1 hdc), 1 hdc into st at base of 2 ch, 1 hdc into each of next 9 hdc, *2 hdc into next hdc, 1 hdc into each of next 9 hdc, rep from * to end, ss to top of 2 ch at beg of round. 110 [121,132] sts.

Round 6: 2 ch (counts as 1 hdc), 1 hdc into each hdc to end, ss to top of 2 ch at beg of round.

ABOVE: In smart blues and greens, this three-color hat could be adapted for any age.

ABOVE: This colorful hat is perfect for a toddler.

Child and adult sizes only

Round 7: 2 ch (counts as 1 hdc), 1 hdc into st at base of 2 ch, 1 hdc into each of next 10 hdc, *2 hdc into next hdc, 1 hdc into each of next 10 hdc, rep from * to end, ss to top of 2 ch at beg of round. [132,144] sts.

Round 8: 2 ch (counts as 1 hdc), 1 hdc into each hdc to end, ss to top of 2 ch at beg of round.

Adult size only

Round 9: 2 ch (counts as 1 hdc), 1 hdc into st at base of 2 ch, 1 hdc into each of next 11 hdc, *2 hdc into next hdc, 1 hdc into each of next 11 hdc, rep from * to end, ss to top of 2 ch at beg of round. 156 sts.

Round 10: 2 ch (counts as 1 hdc), 1 hdc into each hdc to end, ss to top of 2 ch at beg of round.

All sizes

Now work one round of crab st (sc worked from left to right, instead of right to left) around lower edge of hat.

Fasten off.

FOUR-COLOR HAT

Work as given for one-color hat but change color every 2 rounds using all 4 colors in sequence.

THREE-COLOR HAT

Work as given for one-color hat but work 2 rounds in each of the three colors.

TWO-COLOR HAT

Work as given for one-color hat but work 4 rounds in each of the two colors.

Stitch Groups

Most crochet stitch patterns are created by combining various stitches and by the positions in which these stitches are worked. There are a few well-known stitch groups that have their own names – shells, picots, clusters, bobbles, popcorns, and puff stitches.

The names given to these stitch groups relate not to the actual stitch used, but to the way the stitches are grouped together. A shell, cluster, or popcorn may contain any number of stitches and these stitches may be of any size.

SHELLS

A shell, or fan, is usually made up of several of the same type of stitch worked into the same place to create a shell- or fan-like effect.

Normally all the stitches that make up the shell will be worked into just one stitch, rather than into a chain space. This helps to hold the base of the shell together, leaving the upper ends of the stitches to fan out (**A**).

PICOT

A picot is basically a loop of chain stitches that sits on the edge of the crochet to form a little knot or bead.

Picots can be made up of any number of chain stitches, although, most commonly, they will contain either three or four chains. This little loop of chains is then secured by working a stitch into the same place as where the picot began. This can be achieved by working a slip stitch into the first of the picot chains or by working a single crochet into the stitch the picot chain sits on (**B**). Take care to read the pattern so that you know exactly how the picots are to be worked.

CLUSTER

A cluster is a group of stitches that are joined together at the top. The effect created is like that of a shell or fan.

Clusters are usually made up of stitches at least as tall as a double crochet, and the base of each stitch that forms the cluster is usually worked into a different stitch. The pattern should explain exactly where the hook should be inserted for each of the stitches making up the cluster. For a cluster, start by working the first stitch of the group up to the point where there are two loops left on the hook. Now work each of the other stitches to exactly the same stage, remembering to insert the hook at the points detailed in the pattern. You will now have one more loop on your hook than there are stitches making up the cluster. A three double crochet cluster will have four loops on the hook at this point. Take the yarn over the hook again and draw this new loop through all the loops on the hook to close the top of the cluster and complete the stitch group (**C**).

A

B

C

BOBBLES

As its name suggests, a crochet bobble will, create a bobble of yarn on the fabric surface (**D**).

Bobbles are worked in exactly the same way as a cluster except all of the stitches that go to make up the bobble will be worked into the same place, thereby pulling together both the top and the bottom of the stitches. To keep the top of a bobble closed, sometimes a chain stitch will be used to secure it.

POPCORNS

Popcorns are similar to a shell but the two sides of the group are bought together to form the stitches into a tiny cup (**E**).

To make a popcorn, work the stitches as detailed in the pattern. They will usually be stitches at least at tall as a double crochet and they will probably all be worked into one stitch. When this first stage is complete, take the hook out of the working loop. Insert the hook back through the top of the first stitch of the popcorn, pick up the working loop again and draw the working loop through the top of the first stitch, thereby bringing together the first and last stitches of the popcorn.

As with a bobble, it is sometimes best to

secure the top of a popcorn by working a chain stitch. Check the pattern you are following to see if this is needed. If a popcorn is being worked on a wrong-side row or round, make sure that the stitches are gently pushed through so that the popcorn stands proud on the right side of the work.

PUFFS

Puffs are similar to bobbles but they generally use half double crochet stitches. The height of the resulting puff is created by extending the size of the loops that are drawn through the work.

Begin by starting to work a half double crochet stitch. Take the yarn round the hook and insert the hook as detailed. Take the yarn over the hook again and draw this loop through the work. The height of the puff is determined by the length of this loop drawn through the work. Repeat this process as many times as required. You will end up with two loops for every half double crochet started plus one extra loop. Now take the yarn over the hook again and draw this new loop through all the loops on the hook to complete the puff. It is sometimes necessary to secure the top of a puff with a chain stitch (**F**).

Where a pattern regularly uses a particular stitch group you may find that the instructions will refer to working "1 cluster into next stitch," rather than spelling it out in full every time. Exactly how this cluster should be worked will be explained in the abbreviations accompanying the pattern. Sometimes two different types of the same stitch group will

appear within one design – you could have a shell of four double crochets (abbreviated to "4 dc shell") in one place but a shell made up of seven double crochets (abbreviated to "7 dc shell") elsewhere. Read the pattern and abbreviations before you begin to be sure you work each stitch group correctly.

THE CRAB STITCH

Almost all crochet is worked from right to left. The exception to this rule is the crab stitch. This is simply single crochet worked in the "wrong" direction, from left to right, instead of right to left. As the stitches are worked back on themselves, they create a neat knotted effect that is often used as an edging. It is not possible to see the "V"s that make up the stitches and, therefore, you will rarely find another line of stitching worked into crab stitch.

Crab stitch can sometimes take a while to get the hang of – mainly because you feel you should be doing something different. It is just single crochet worked from left to right, instead of right to left.

1. Insert the hook into the next stitch from front to back in exactly the way you would normally – but use the stitch to the right, not the left, twisting the hook back on itself.
2. Wrap the yarn around the hook in the normal way and draw this loop through the work (**G**). Take the yarn over the hook again and draw this loop through both loops on the hook to complete the stitch.

Fashion Scarves

Combine a lacy stitch with luxury yarn to make these cozy scarves. Choose either the fluffy version for casual wear, or the sophisticated shorter version in silk for a smart look.

MEASUREMENTS

Long scarf is approx 8½ inches wide and
71 inches long (excluding fringe)
Short scarf is approx 8 inches wide and
45¼ inches long

MATERIALS

For the long scarf:
Rowan Kid Soft (1¾ oz. per ball): 4 balls
in magenta
Size H crochet hook

For the short scarf:
Jaeger Silk 4 ply (1¾ oz. per ball): 3 balls
in purple
Size C crochet hook

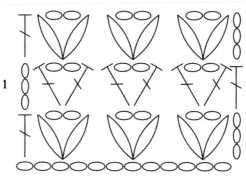

KEY

⬯ ch

🇹 dc

⬮ cluster

GAUGE

Long scarf (above): 4 patt repeats (16 sts)
to 4¼ inches and 12 rows to 4½ inches using
a size H hook, or size required to give correct
gauge.
Short scarf (below): 9 patt repeats (36 sts)
to 5 inches and 16 rows to 6 inches using size
E hook, or size required to give correct gauge.

ABBREVIATIONS

cluster = *yo and insert hook as indicated,
yo and draw loop through lengthening loop to
approx ⅜ inch for long scarf or just over ¼
inch for short scarf, yo and draw through 2
loops on hook, rep from * once more, yo and
draw through 2 loops on hook, yo and draw
through last 2 loops on hook.
Also see page 11.

ABOVE: This diagram shows the stitches used for both scarves.

LONG SCARF

Using a size H hook, make 35 ch.

Foundation row: Skip 4 ch (counts as 1 dc and 1 ch), *(1 cluster, 2 ch and 1 cluster) into next ch, skip 3 ch, rep from * to last 3 ch, (1 cluster, 2 ch and 1 cluster) into next ch, skip 1 ch, 1 dc into last ch, turn. 8 patt repeats, 34 sts.

Now work in patt as follows:

Row 1: 3 ch (counts as 1 dc), (1 dc, 2 ch and 1 dc) into each ch sp to end, 1 dc into top of turning ch, turn.

Row 2: 3 ch (counts as 1 dc), (1 cluster, 2 ch and 1 cluster) into each ch sp to end, 1 dc into top of turning ch, turn.

Rows 1 and 2 form patt.

Cont in patt until scarf measures 71 inches, ending after patt row 2.

Fasten off.

For fringe, cut 12-inch lengths of yarn and knot pairs of threads across short ends of scarf, positioning each knot of fringe in corners of scarf and between each pair of clusters.

Do not press.

SHORT SCARF

Using a size C hook, make 59 ch.

Work foundation row as for Long Scarf.

14 patt repeats, 58 sts.

Beg with patt row 1, work in patt as for Long Scarf until work measures 45¼ inches, ending after patt row 2.

Do NOT fasten off.

Edging round: Working down adjacent row end edge, work 3 ch, 1 sc around dc at end of last row, *3 ch, 1 sc around 3 ch at beg of previous row, 3 ch, 1 sc around dc at end of previous row, rep from * until sc has been worked around dc at end of foundation row, 3 ch, 1 sc into same place as last sc, now working across foundation ch edge, work *3 ch, skip ch at base of clusters, (1 sc, 3 ch and 1 sc) into next ch sp, rep from * until both sc have been worked into ch sp at beg of foundation row, cont in this way until all four edges have been completed, replacing "sc" at end of last rep with "ss to first sc".

Fasten off.

Press lightly.

Working an Edging

Although the row ends of a piece of crochet can be very neat, they often look better if a separate edging is worked along them. This will smooth out the edge and create a finished look.

When adding an edging to a piece of crochet, it is best to use a size or two smaller hook than the one used for the main sections. As the edging is there to hold the row ends in shape and avoid stretching, work it so that it just gently pulls the edge in slightly.

WORKING ACROSS THE TOP OF A ROW

When working across the top of a row of crochet, work the edging into the stitches in the same way as you would if working another row (**A**).

When working across the foundation chain edge, insert the hook under the remaining loop of each of the foundation chain stitches.

Depending on the stitch pattern used for both the main section and the edging, you may find it necessary to either decrease or increase the number of stitches worked. As a crochet edging is very flexible, there is no real hard and fast rule as to how many stitches to work for an edging. The right number is the amount that sits properly. You may find it easier to try out the edging on your gauge swatch to work out the correct number of stitches you will need for the edging to sit correctly.

WORKING ALONG ROW ENDS

When working along row ends, place the stitches an even distance apart along the edge and the same distance in from the finished edge. Try to work the same number of stitches in each pair of row ends – as a guide, a single crochet edging worked along the sides of a double crochet fabric would need roughly three stitches for every two rows. Again, position the stitches so that they hold the edge in slightly (**B**).

If the edge is still wavy and too full after the first row or round of an edging has been completed, it will probably get worse once the rest of it has been worked. Take time at this point to unpick the first row or round and re-do it.

WORKING ALONG A CURVED EDGE

Working an edging along a curved edge will require varying numbers of stitches in each row, or round, to maintain a flat and smooth edging.

On an internal curve – such as a neck edge – work fewer stitches as required on each row or round by simply skipping a stitch at even points along the edge (**C**).

On an external curve, you will need to add a few stitches to give the extra length needed. Do this by simply working twice into stitches as required (**D**).

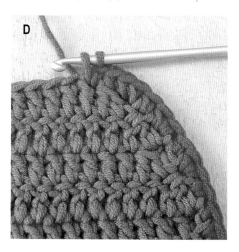

The amount of stitches you will need to add or lose will vary depending on how tight the curve is and the height of the stitch being used for the edging. Again, trial and error is the only sure-fire way of getting an edging to sit correctly.

Working an edging around a corner requires extra stitches to be added at the corner to allow the edging to turn without distorting the work (**E**).

E

As a guide, corners are normally turned by working three stitches into the actual corner point on most rows. Again, the number of times that extra stitches are added and how many are actually added will depend on the height of the stitch being used. You will obviously need more stitches to turn a corner with trebles than with single crochet.

MAKING SEPARATE CROCHET EDGINGS

Crochet is also well suited to making a separate lacy edging that is sewn on to a ready-made item (**F**). These edgings can either be made lengthwise, working as long a length as required on a few stitches, or widthwise, by working just a few rows on the number of stitches needed to fit the edge.

Whichever way the edging is made, it is a good idea to make it slightly longer than it appears to need. Crochet has a tendency to pull back in on itself and the edging, therefore, needs to have a little extra fullness to it. As a rough guide, add about an extra 2–3 inches for every yard of edging.

When calculating the amount of edging you need, remember to allow extra to turn any corners. Add twice the finished width of the edging extra at each corner. And, if the edging is to go around a circular mat or cloth, remember to add enough so that it will lie flat. This extra length can be gently eased in as the edging is sewn in place. If possible, sew it as you make it, adding to the length as needed as you go along.

F

ATTACHING A CROCHET EDGING

Attaching a crochet edging to a ready-made item is best done by hand.

1. Place the edging and the item to be trimmed together, right sides facing, so that the inner (usually straight) edge of the edging matches the finished edge. Use a shade of sewing thread that complements the edging (we have used a contrasting color here to illustrate the stitches) and very neatly slip stitch the inner edge of the edging in place to the outer edge of the item it is to trim. Work small, neat stitches, placing them close together so that the edging is securely held in place (**G**). Ease in any fullness as necessary as you stitch.

G

2. Once completed, fold the edging away from the item and press it carefully. The stitching, if worked correctly, should be virtually invisible.

Pressing and Blocking

Once a piece of crochet has been completed, it should be pressed. The way to do this will vary, depending on the type of item you are making and the yarn that you have used.

Remember – pressing is very different from ironing. When ironing, the iron slides around on the fabric surface. When pressing, the iron is gently lowered on to – or held just above – the fabric for a second or two and then lifted away. It never slides over the surface.

Whatever yarn has been used, refer to the ball band to see how the manufacturer recommends pressing it. Regardless of the directions given on the ball band, it is always a good idea to cover the work with a pressing cloth to avoid any chance of damaging the surface of the work.

If the surface of the work is textured, sometimes it is better to simply block out the pieces, rather than press them. To block out a piece of crochet, you will need a flat, firm, but soft surface that is larger than the crocheted piece – an ironing board or a table covered with soft towels is suitable.

Lay the crochet section on to this surface, with the right side uppermost, and gently ease the crochet into shape. Pin the edges of the crochet in place, placing the pins at regular but close intervals along the edges. Make sure that you have pinned it square on to the surface, and double-check the size.

Once you are satisfied that everything is pinned in place, the crochet can be dampened. This can be done either by gently spraying with water from a spray bottle or by covering the work with a damp cloth. Leave the pinned pieces in place to dry naturally before removing the cloth and pins. If necessary, the sections can then be joined to complete the work.

Circular lacy items that are supposed to lie flat are often nowhere near their finished size and are in no way flat when the crochet work has been completed. These items need to be blocked, or pinned out on to a firm surface, flattening and stretching them to size. The design will often feature points around the outer edge – place the pins at these points to accentuate them. As a general rule, as the item is stretched to size, it will flatten out. If you are making a mat or cloth where the finished size is not vital and you cannot stretch it out to the specified size, simple adjust the pin positions so that the item is smooth at a comfortable size to show the stitches off well.

Once the item is stretched to size and pinned securely in place, it can either be pressed or blocked. Sometimes it may be necessary to use a combination of the two methods as pressing will help ease in any fullness stopping the center from lying flat. If you want a fairly rigid crisp finish to the work, replace the water spray with spray starch. Whatever method is used, remember not to remove the pins until the item is completely dry.

Heirloom Bedspread

Create your own heirloom and add a touch of Victoriana to your home with this traditional-style, crisp-white bedspread. It is made up of a number of squares joined together.

MEASUREMENTS

Finished twin-size bedspread is 68½ inches by 92 inches.
Finished full-size bedspread is 84¼ inches by 92 inches.

MATERIALS

Rowan Handknit DK Cotton in white (Bleached 263) (1¾ oz. per ball): 84 balls for twin size, or 104 balls for double size
Size E crochet hook

GAUGE

One square measures 8 inches using a size E hook, or size required to give correct gauge.

ABBREVIATIONS

popcorn = work 5 dc into same place, take hook out of working loop, insert it through top of first of these 5 dc, pick up working loop again and draw through top of first dc to close top of popcorn. Make sure popcorn projects out on to right side of work. Also see page 11.

SQUARE

Using size E hook, make 6 ch and join with a ss to form a ring.
Round 1: 3 ch, 4 dc into ring, take hook out of working loop, insert it through top of 3 ch at beg of round, pick up working loop again and draw through top of 3 ch to close top of starting popcorn, (5 ch, 1 popcorn into ring) 3 times, 5 ch, ss to top of starting popcorn.
Round 2: 3 ch (counts as 1 dc), *(2 dc, 2 ch, 1 popcorn, 2 ch and 2 dc) into next ch sp**,

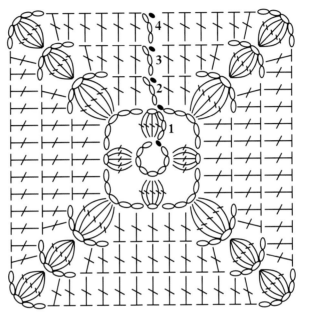

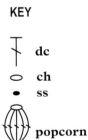

LEFT: This stitch diagram shows the first four rounds of each square that makes up the bedspread.

KEY

┬	dc
◯	ch
●	ss
(popcorn symbol)	popcorn

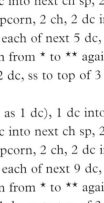

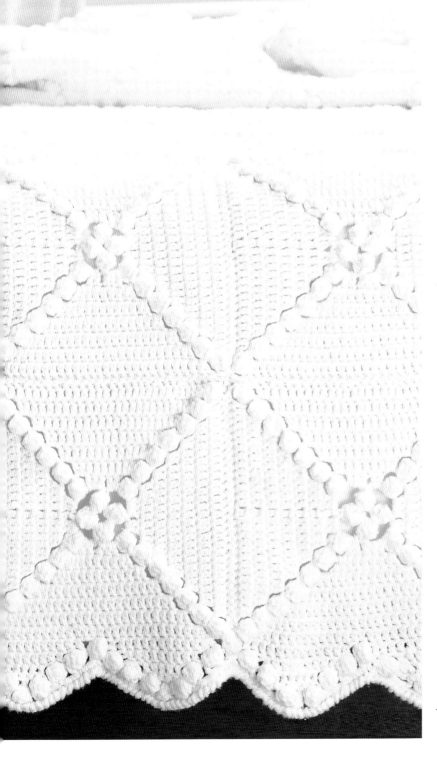

1 dc into next popcorn, rep from * twice more, then from * to ** again, ss to top of 3 ch at beg of round.

Round 3: 3 ch (counts as 1 dc), 1 dc into each of next 2 dc, *2 dc into next ch sp, 2 ch, 1 popcorn into next popcorn, 2 ch, 2 dc into next ch sp**, 1 dc into each of next 5 dc, rep from * twice more, then from * to ** again, 1 dc into each of next 2 dc, ss to top of 3 ch at beg of round.

Round 4: 3 ch (counts as 1 dc), 1 dc into each of next 4 dc, *2 dc into next ch sp, 2 ch, 1 popcorn into next popcorn, 2 ch, 2 dc into next ch sp**, 1 dc into each of next 9 dc, rep from * twice more, then from * to ** again, 1 dc into each of next 4 dc, ss to top of 3 ch at beg of round.

Round 5: 3 ch (counts as 1 dc), 1 dc into each of next 6 dc, *2 dc into next ch sp, 2 ch, 1 popcorn into next popcorn, 2 ch, 2 dc into next ch sp**, 1 dc into each of next 13 dc, rep from * twice more, then from * to ** again, 1 dc into each of next 6 dc, ss to top of 3 ch at beg of round.

Round 6: 3 ch (counts as 1 dc), 1 dc into each of next 8 dc, *2 dc into next ch sp, 2 ch, 1 popcorn into next popcorn, 2 ch, 2 dc into next ch sp**, 1 dc into each of next 17 dc, rep from * twice more, then from * to ** again, 1 dc into each of next 8 dc, ss to top of 3 ch at beg of round.

Round 7: 3 ch (counts as 1 dc), 1 dc into each of next 10 dc, *2 dc into next ch sp, 2 ch, 1 popcorn into next popcorn, 2 ch, 2 dc into next ch sp**, 1 dc into each of next 21 dc, rep from * twice more, then from * to ** again, 1 dc into each of next 10 dc, ss to top of 3 ch at beg of round.

Round 8: 3 ch (counts as 1 dc), 1 dc into each of next 12 dc, *2 dc into next ch sp, 2 ch, 1 popcorn into next popcorn, 2 ch, 2 dc into next ch sp**, 1 dc into each of next 25 dc, rep from * twice more, then from * to ** again, 1 dc into each of next 12 dc, ss to top of 3 ch at beg of round.

Fasten off.

Completed square has a popcorn in each corner, 2 ch on each side of this popcorn and 29 dc along sides between corners.

CENTER SECTION

For a twin-size bedspread, make 88 squares.
For a full-size bedspread, make 110 squares.
Join squares to form Center Section as follows: Hold two squares together with right
sides facing and work a row of sc along the
joining edge, working 1 sc for each popcorn,
ch or dc and inserting hook for each sc
through top of relevant st on both squares.
Fasten off. Join squares to form 11 strips of 8
squares for single bedspread, or 10 squares
for double bedspread, then join strips to form
a rectangle 11 squares long by 8 squares wide
for single bedspread, or 10 squares wide for
double bedspread.

EDGING

Using a size E hook, rejoin yarn at one point
where squares have been joined and, with
right side facing, work edging all round

Center Section as follows:

Round 1: 3 ch, 4 dc into joining point, take
hook out of working loop, insert it through
top of 3 ch at beg of round, pick up working
loop again and draw through top of 3 ch to
close top of starting popcorn, *1 ch, skip
2 ch, 1 dc into each of next 13 dc, 1 ch, skip
1 dc, 1 popcorn into next dc, 1 ch, skip 1 dc,
1 dc into each of next 13 dc, 1 ch, skip 2 ch,
1 popcorn into next joining point, rep from *
to end, working popcorn into corner
popcorns at all four corners of Center
Section and omitting popcorn at end of last
rep, ss to top of starting popcorn.

Now work each point of Edging separately.

Row 2: 3 ch, skip popcorn at base of 3 ch
and next 1 ch, 1 popcorn into next dc, 1 ch,
skip 1 dc, 1 dc into each of next 9 dc, 1 ch,
skip 1 dc, 1 popcorn into next dc, skip 1 ch,
1 dc into top of next popcorn (mark this

popcorn), turn.

Row 3 – 3 ch, skip first popcorn and next 1 ch, 1 popcorn into next dc, 1 ch, skip 1 dc, 1 dc into each of next 5 dc, 1 ch, skip 1 dc, 1 popcorn into next dc, skip 1 ch, 1 dc into top of next popcorn, turn.

Row 4: 3 ch, skip first popcorn and next 1 ch, 1 popcorn into next dc, 1 ch, skip 1 dc, 1 dc into next dc, 1 ch, skip 1 dc, 1 popcorn into next dc, skip 1 ch, 1 dc into top of next popcorn, turn.

Row 5: 3 ch, skip first popcorn and next 1 ch, 1 popcorn into next dc, skip 1 ch, 1 dc into top of next popcorn.

Fasten off.

First point of Edging completed.

With right side facing, re-join yarn to marked popcorn and work rows 2 to 5 again.

Continue in this way until points have been worked all round Center Section.

With right side facing, re-join yarn to outer edge and work one round of sc all round points of Edging, working 3 sc into each 3 ch sp along sides of points and 1 sc into popcorn at top of point, and ending with ss to first sc, do NOT turn.

Now work one round of crab stitch (sc worked from left to right, not right to left) around entire outer edge, ending with ss to first sc.

Fasten off.

Finishing

Carefully press from wrong side, using a warm iron over a damp cloth. Work on a soft but firm surface (such as several layers of towels laid over an ironing board). Once complete, gently ease any popcorns that may have slipped through to the wrong side back through to the right side of the work.

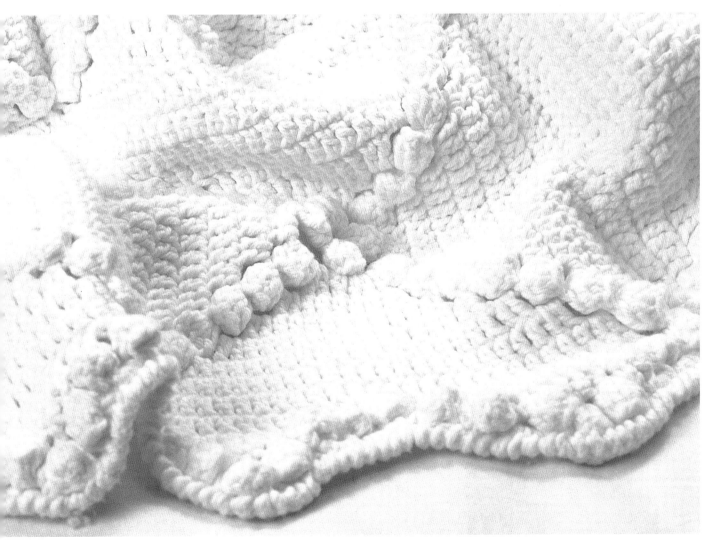

Elegant Edging

Enhance sheets and pillowcases with this simple but effective lacy edging. Quick and easy to crochet, this trimming can be made to any length required.

MEASUREMENTS

Finished edging is approx 1¼ inches wide

MATERIALS

Coats Aida 5 Crochet Cotton (1¾ oz. per ball) in white (color 1): one ball will be sufficient for approx 102 inches of edging
No. 5 steel crochet hook
Needle and thread

GAUGE

One pattern repeat (4 rows) measures 1 inch using a No. 5 steel hook, or size required to give correct gauge.

ABBREVIATIONS

See page 11.

EDGING

Using a No. 5 steel hook, make 6 ch.
Foundation row: 1 dc into 4th ch from hook, 1 dc into each of next 2 ch, turn. 4 sts.
Now work in patt as follows:
Row 1: 3 ch (counts as 1 dc), skip first st, 1 dc into each of rem 3 sts, working last dc into top of turning ch, turn.
Row 2: As row 1.
Row 3: 3 ch (counts as 1 dc), skip first st, 1 dc into each of next 2 dc, (1 dc – mark this dc, 4 ch and 1 sc) into top of turning ch, 7 ch, working along row end edges 1 sc into same place as last dc of row 1, 2 ch, 1 dc into corresponding point along row edge but one row lower, turn.
Row 4: Skip (1 dc, 2 ch and 1 sc), [1 ch, 1 dc into next ch sp] 6 times, 1 ch, skip 1 sc, 1 sc into next ch sp, ss along and into marked

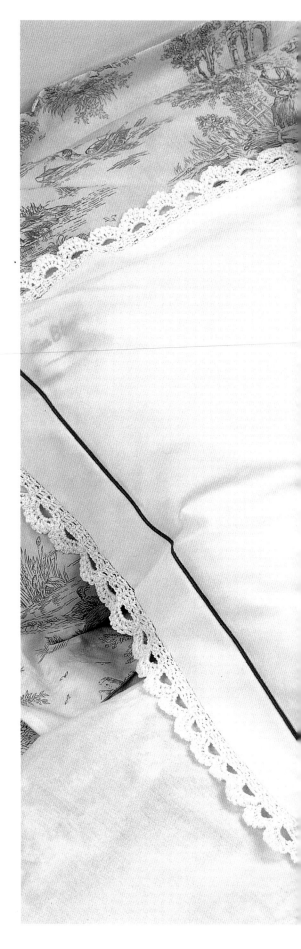

dc, 3 ch (counts as 1 dc), 1 dc into each of rem 3 sts, working last dc into top of turning ch, turn.

These 4 rows form patt.

Cont in patt until Edging is required length, ending after patt row 3.

Next row: Skip (1 dc, 2 ch and 1 sc), [1 ch, 1 dc into next ch sp] 6 times, 1 ch, skip 1 sc, 1 sc into next ch sp, turn.

Along edge of each scallop there are 9 ch sps – work into these ch sps for the edging row. Now work along outer edge of scallops as follows:

Edging row: Skip sc at end of last row, ⋆[1 sc into next ch sp, 4 ch] 6 times, 1 sc into next ch sp (this is 8th ch sp of this scallop)⋆⋆, 1 ch, skip last ch sp of this scallop and first ch sp of next scallop, rep from ⋆ to end, ending last rep at ⋆⋆.

Fasten off.

Finishing

Press carefully. Pin edging in place to fabric edges, then neatly sew straight edge to outer edge of fabric, gathering edging to fit around corners, joining ends of edging if necessary.

Baby Cardigan, Hat, and Blanket

The pretty textured flowers make this adorable baby sweater, hat, and blanket extra special. Choose soft pastel colors for your new arrival.

MEASUREMENTS

To fit age	0-3	3-6	6-12	12-18 months
Chest	16	18	20	22 inches

CARDIGAN

Actual size	18½	20½	22½	24½ inches
Length	8¼	10	11½	13 inches
Sleeve seam	5	6¼	8	10¼ inches

HAT

Width around head	12	13¾	13¾	15¾ inches

BLANKET

Finished size	27 x 35 inches

MATERIALS

Sirdar Country Style 4 ply (1¾ oz. per ball):

For cardigan and hat:

MS – white	1	1	2	2 balls
A – pink	1	1	1	1 balls
B – blue	1	1	1	1 balls

Size C crochet hook
4 buttons

For blanket:

MS – white	6 balls
A – pink	3 balls
B – blue	3 balls

Size C crochet hook

GAUGE

23 sts and 12½ rows to 4 inches measured over double crochet fabric using a size C hook, or size required to give correct gauge. Motif measures 2 inches square.

ABBREVIATIONS

dc2tog = *yo and insert into next st, yo and draw loop through, yo and draw through 2 loops, rep from * once more, yo and draw through all 3 loops on hook.
See also page 11.

FLOWER MOTIF

Using a size C hook and first color (either pink or blue), make 5 ch and join with a ss to form a ring.

Round 1: *2 ch, (4 dc and 1 ss) into ring, rep from * twice more.

Round 2: Working behind petals of round 1, skip 2 ch at beg of previous round, 1 sc into

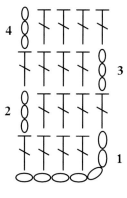

LEFT: This stitch diagram shows the double crochet fabric used for the main sections of the cardigan and hat.

KEY

┼   **dc**

◯   **ch**

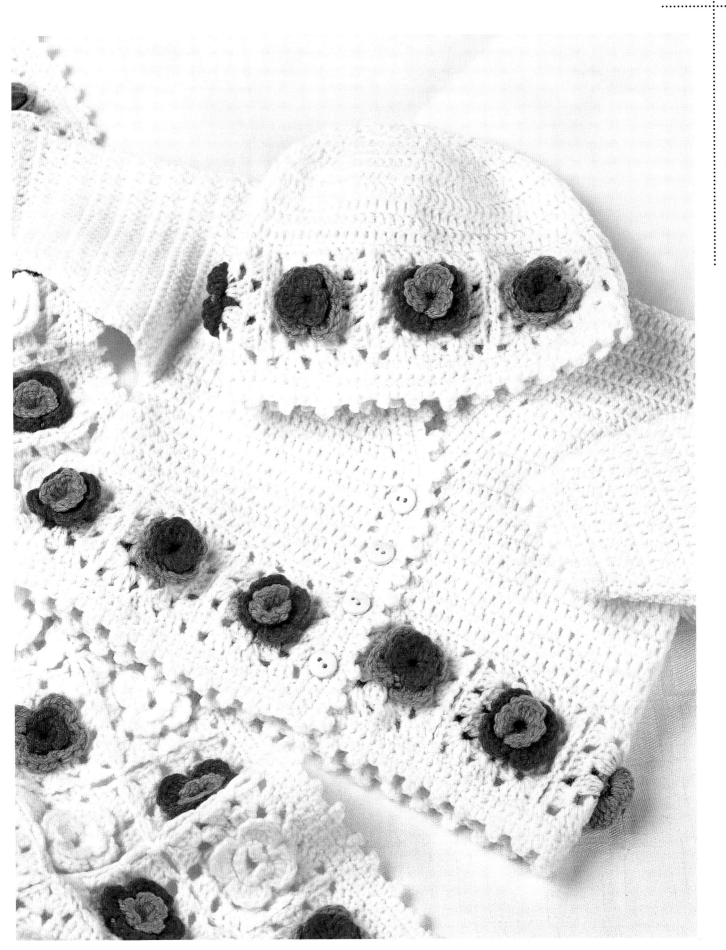

foundation ring, 2 ch, skip 3 dc, 1 sc into ring, 2 ch, skip (1 dc, 1 ss, 2 ch and 2 dc), 1 sc into foundation ring, 2 ch, skip (2 dc, 1 ss, 2 ch and 1 dc), 1 sc into foundation ring, 2 ch, skip (3 dc and 1 ss), ss to first sc.

Break off first color and join in second color.

Round 3: (1 ss, 5 dc and 1 ss) into each ch sp of previous round.

Round 4: Working behind petals of round 3, 1 ch, *inserting hook from back and from right to left work 1 sc around stem of sc of round 2, 4 ch, rep from * 3 times more, ss to first sc.

Break off second color and join in MS.

Round 5: Ss into first ch sp, 3 ch (counts as first dc), (2 dc, 3 ch and 3 dc) into same ch sp, *1 ch, (3 dc, 3 ch and 3 dc) into next ch sp, rep from * twice more, 1 sc into 3rd of 3 ch at beg of round.

Round 6: 3 ch (counts as first dc), 2 dc into sp formed by sc at end of previous round, *1 ch, (3 dc, 3 ch and 3 dc) into next ch sp, 1 ch**, 3 dc into next ch sp, rep from * twice more and then from * to ** again, ss to 3rd of 3 ch at beg of round.

Fasten off.

Each motif is a square and has one 3 ch sp in each corner and two 1 ch sps along each side. The motifs are joined to form the final pieces whilst working round 6. Replace the (3 ch) at each corner with (1 ch, 1 sc into corresponding corner sp on Motif to be joined, 1 ch), and the (1 ch) along sides with (1 sc into corresponding 1 ch sp on Motif to be joined).

CARDIGAN

BODY (worked in one piece to armholes)

Motif Border

Make and join a strip of 9 [10,11,12] Motifs as follows: use A as first color and B as second color on First Motif, B as first color and A as second color on Second Motif, and cont in this way, alternating colors at centers.

Hem Border

With RS facing, using a size C hook and MS, work 103 [115,127,139] sc evenly along lower edge of Motif Border (this is 11 sc for each motif plus an extra 4 [5,6,7] sc evenly distributed along edge), turn.

Row 1: (WS), 1 ch (does NOT count as st), 1 sc into each sc to end, turn.

Row 2: As row 1.

Row 3: 1 ch (does NOT count as st), 1 sc into each of first 2 sc, *3 ch, ss to top of last sc, 1 sc into each of next 3 sc, rep from * to last 2 sc, 3 ch, ss to top of last sc, 1 sc into each of last 2 sc.

Fasten off.

Main Section

With RS facing, using a size C hook and MS, work 103 [115,127,139] sc evenly along upper edge of Motif Border (this is 11 sc for each motif plus an extra 4 [5,6,7] sc evenly distributed along edge), turn.

Row 1: 3 ch (counts as first st), 1 dc into each st to end, turn.

This row forms double crochet fabric.

Cont in double crochet fabric until Main Section measures 4 [5,6¼,7½] inches from lower edge.

Divide for armholes

Next row: 3 ch (counts as first st), dc2tog over next 2 sts, 1 dc into each of next 22 [25,28,31] dc, turn.

Work on this set of 24 [27,30,33] sts only for first front.

Next row: 3 ch (counts as first st), 1 dc into each dc to last 3 sts, dc2tog over next 2 sts, 1 dc into last st, turn.

Working all decreases as set by last 2 rows, dec 1 st at front slope edge of next 3 [4,5,6] rows, then on every foll alt row until 17 [19,21,23] sts rem.

Work a few rows even until armhole measures 4¼ [4¾,5,5½] inches.

Fasten off.

Shape back

Return to last complete row worked, rejoin yarn to next dc with RS facing and proceed as follows:

Next row: 3 ch (counts as first st), 1 dc into each of next 52 [58,64,70] dc, turn.

Cont on these 53 [59,65,71] sts only until back matches first front to shoulder.

Fasten off.

Shape second front

Return to last complete row worked, rejoin yarn to next dc with RS facing and proceed as follows:

Next row – 3 ch (counts as first st), 1 dc into each dc to last 3 sts, dc2tog over next 2 sts, 1 dc into last st, turn.

Complete second front to match first, reversing shapings.

SLEEVES
Main Section

Using a size C hook and MS, make 31 [33,35,37] ch.

Row 1: 1 dc into 4th ch from hook, 1 dc into each ch to end, turn. 29 [31,33,35] sts.

Row 2: 3 ch (counts as first st), 2 dc into next dc, 1 dc into dc to last 2 sts, 2 dc into next st, 1 dc into last st, turn. 31 [33,35,37] sts.

Working all increases as set by last row, inc 1 st at each end of next 10 [10,6,1] rows, then on foll 0 [1,6,12] alt rows. 51 [55,59,63] sts.

Work a few rows even until Sleeve measures 4¼ [5½,7,9½] inches.

Fasten off.

Cuff

With RS facing, using a size C hook and MS, work 28 [31,34,34] sc evenly along foundation ch edge of Sleeve, turn.

Work rows 1 to 3 as given for Hem Border of Body.
Fasten off.

FINISHING
Join shoulder seams.
Front and Neck Edging
Mark positions for 4 buttonholes along right front opening edge – top button level with start of front slope shaping, lowest buttonhole ½ inch above lower edge and rem 2 buttonholes evenly spaced between.
With RS facing, using a size C hook and MS, rejoin yarn at base of right front opening edge and, working a multiple of 3 sts, work a row of sc up right front opening edge to shoulder, across back neck and down left front opening edge to lower edge, turn.

Row 1: (WS), 1 ch (does NOT count as st), 1 sc into each sc to end, making buttonholes to correspond with positions marked for buttonholes by replacing (1 sc into each of next 2 sc) with (2 ch, skip 2 sc) and working 2 sc into sc at corner points at beg of front slope shaping, turn.

Row 2: 1 ch (does NOT count as st), 1 sc into each sc to end, working 2 sc into each buttonhole ch sp, turn.

Row 3: 1 ch (does NOT count as st), 1 sc into first sc, ⋆3 ch, ss to top of last sc, 1 sc into each of next 3 sc, rep from ⋆ to last sc, 3 ch, ss to top of last sc, 1 sc into last sc.
Fasten off.
Join sleeve seams. Sew sleeves into armholes.
Sew on buttons.

HAT
Motif Border
Make and join a strip of 6 [7,7,8] Motifs as follows: use A as first color and B as second color on First Motif, B as first color and A as second color on Second Motif, and cont in this way, alternating colors at centers.

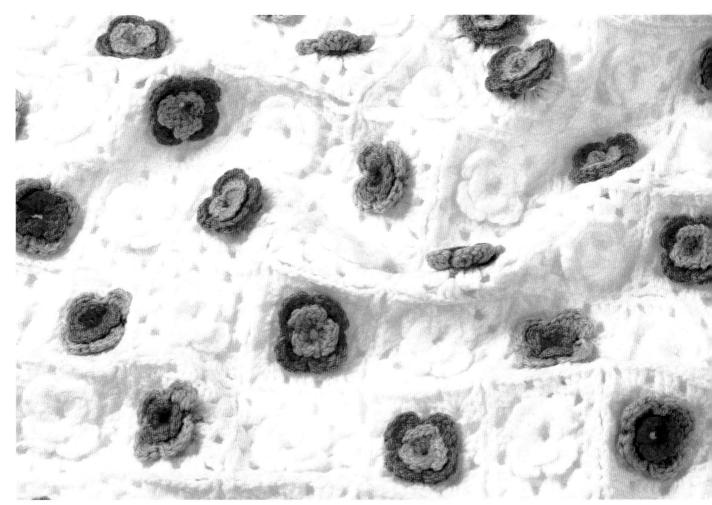

Hem Border

With RS facing, using a size C hook and MS, work 67 [79,79,91] sc evenly along lower edge of Motif Border (this is 11 sc for each motif plus an extra 1 [2,2,3] evenly distributed along edge sc), turn.

Row 1: (WS), 1 ch (does NOT count as st), 1 sc into each sc to end, turn.

Row 2: As row 1.

Row 3: 1 ch (does NOT count as st), 1 sc into each of first 2 sc, *3 ch, ss to top of last sc, 1 sc into each of next 3 sc, rep from * to last 2 sc, 3 ch, ss to top of last sc, 1 sc into each of last 2 sc.
Fasten off.

Main Section

With RS facing, using a size C hook and MS, work 67 [78,78,89] sc evenly along upper edge of Motif Border (this is 11 sc for each motif plus an extra 1 sc), turn.

Row 1: 3 ch (counts as first st), 1 dc into each st to end, turn. This row forms double crochet fabric. Cont in double crochet fabric until Main Section measures 3½ [4,4¼,4¾] inches from lower edge.

Shape crown

Row 1: 3 ch (counts as first st), (dc2tog over next 2 sts, 1 dc into each of next 9 dc) 6 [7,7,8] times, turn. 61 [71,71,81] sts.

Row 2: 3 ch (counts as first st), (dc2tog over next 2 sts, 1 dc into each of next 3 dc) 12 [14,14,16] times, turn. 49 [57,57,65] sts.

Row 3: 3 ch (counts as first st), (dc2tog over next 2 sts, 1 dc into each of next 2 dc) 12 [14,14,16] times, turn. 37 [43,43,49] sts.

Row 4: 3 ch (counts as first st), (dc2tog over next 2 sts, 1 dc into next dc) 12 [14,14,16] times, turn. 25 [29,29,33] sts.

Row 5: 3 ch (counts as first st), (dc2tog over next 2 sts) 12 [14,14,16] times, turn. 13 [15,15,17] sts.

Row 6: 3 ch (counts as first st), (dc2tog over

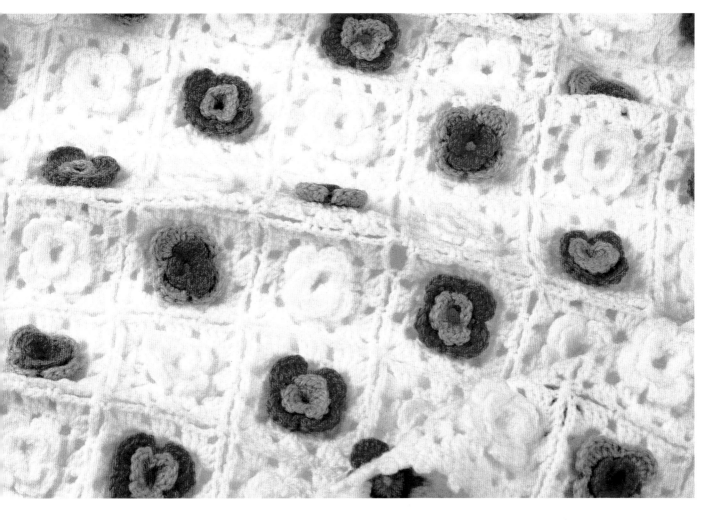

RIGHT: Follow this chart for the correct positioning of the motifs on the baby blanket.

A	B	A	C	A	B	A	B	A	C	A	B	A
B	A	C	A	B	A	C	A	B	A	C	A	B
A	C	A	B	A	C	A	C	A	B	A	C	A
C	A	B	A	C	A	B	A	C	A	B	A	C
A	B	A	C	A	B	A	B	A	C	A	B	A
B	A	C	A	B	A	C	A	B	A	C	A	B
A	C	A	B	A	C	A	C	A	B	A	C	A
C	A	B	A	C	A	B	A	C	A	B	A	C
A	B	A	C	A	B	A	B	A	C	A	B	A
C	A	B	A	C	A	B	A	C	A	B	A	C
A	C	A	B	A	C	A	C	A	B	A	C	A
B	A	C	A	B	A	C	A	B	A	C	A	B
A	B	A	C	A	B	A	B	A	C	A	B	A
C	A	B	A	C	A	B	A	C	A	B	A	C
A	C	A	B	A	C	A	C	A	B	A	C	A
B	A	C	A	B	A	C	A	B	A	C	A	B
A	B	A	C	A	B	A	B	A	C	A	B	A

A = work all rounds of motif using Main Shade

B = use A as 1st color, B as 2nd color and work rest of motif in Main Shade

C = use B as 1st color, A as 2nd color and work rest of motif in Main Shade

next 2 sts) 6 [7,7,8] times, turn. 7 [8,8,9] sts.
Fasten off.
Join back seam.

BLANKET
Main Section
Make and join 221 Motifs to form a rectangle
13 motifs wide by 17 motifs long, using colors as indicated on diagram opposite.

Border
With RS facing, using a size C hook and MS,
work 1 row of sc evenly all round outer edge
of Main Section, working 11 sc along sides of
each motif and an extra 1 sc in each corner,
ss to first sc, turn. 664 sts.
Round 1: (WS), 1 ch (does NOT count as st),
1 sc into each sc to end, working 3 sc into
each corner sc and ending with ss to first
sc, turn. 672 sts.
Round 2: As round 1. 680 sts.
Round 3: 1 ch (does NOT count as st),
1 sc into first sc, *3 ch, ss to top of last sc,
1 sc into each of next 3 sc, rep from * to last
sc, 3 ch, ss to top of last sc, 1 sc into last sc,
ss to first sc.
Fasten off.

Finishing
Carefully press from wrong side, using a
cool iron over a dry cloth. Work on a soft
but firm surface (such as several layers of
towels laid over an ironing board). Gently
ease the flowers of each motif into shape.

Placing the Stitches

The textured effects that appear in crochet are formed in a variety of ways. You can either make them by working the basic stitches in combinations that create the texture, or you can vary the points where the base of the stitches are placed.

When creating a textured effect by varying the placement of the stitches, the actual stitch will be made in exactly the same way as would normally be the case. It is only the point where the hook is inserted through the previous rows or rounds that changes. Check the pattern you are following to find out exactly how to place the stitches.

WORKING INTO THE TOPS OF STITCHES

Insert the hook from the front under both loops of the "V" at the top of the stitch being worked (**A**). This is the standard way to insert the hook for all the basic crochet stitches. All stitches should be worked in this manner unless the pattern specifies otherwise.

A

WORKING THROUGH ONE LOOP

By working the new stitches through just one of the loops of the "V," a line is left across the work (**B**). This line forms a slight ridge and, by alternating the loop that is left unworked – either the front or back loop – a basket-weave effect can be created.

B

When crocheting in rows, working into the same (front or back) loop of every stitch of every row with leave a ridge on the front of the work for one row and at the back of the work for the next row. If you want the ridges to appear on one particular side for every row, the loop used for the stitch must be alternated. For example, use the front loop for all right side rows and the back loop for every wrong side row.

Similarly, when working in rounds, working into the same (front or back) loop for every round will leave the ridge on the same side of the work throughout. If the ridge is to alternately appear on both sides of the work, the loop used for the stitch must be alternated on every round.

WORKING INTO CHAIN SPACES

Placing the new stitches into a chain space (**abbreviated to "ch sp"**), rather than working into the actual chain stitches, completely encloses the chain. The stitches are worked in the normal way but, instead of inserting the hook under the two bars of the "V," it is inserted into the chain space (**C**).

C

Rarely will you find the same number of stitches worked into a chain space as there are chains making up the space. Many lacy patterns will work just one stitch into a chain space, to create a mesh effect, or many stitches, to shape the work or form a particular stitch group.

WORKING BETWEEN STITCHES

Placing new stitches between the stitches of a previous row, or round, will create a slightly lacy effect as the old stitches are gently eased apart.

Insert the hook from the front, taking great care to insert the hook between the stitches without accidentally picking up a strand of one of them (**D**).

D

A stitch worked in this way will add less height to the work than one worked into the top of a row or round. This is because the base of the stitch is below the top of the previous row.

RELIEF STITCHES

Instead of working into a stitch, it is possible to work around the body of the stitch, between the point where it joins the previous row and the top where the "V" will be visible. Because of the heavily textured effect this creates, this type of stitch is known as a relief stitch. Although, within reason, it is possible to work any height of relief stitch. A relief double crochet is the most commonly used type.

Relief stitches create very heavily textured fabrics that can be reversible. The crochet stitches are also quite tightly packed on each other so a lot of yarn is used –- but they form a thick, warm fabric that is ideal for outerwear, and blankets and throws.

To work a relief front-double crochet (**abbreviated to "rfdc"**), wrap the yarn around the hook and then insert it from the front and from the right to the left around the stem of the stitch of the previous row. Wrap the yarn around the hook in the usual way and draw this loop through from the beginning of the stem of the stitch being worked

E

(**E**). Now complete the double crochet in the normal way.

To work a relief back-double crochet (**abbreviated to "rbdc"**), wrap the yarn around the hook and insert the hook into the work from the back and from the right to the left around the stem of the stitch of the previous row. Wrap the yarn around the hook in

F

the normal way and draw this new loop through the work (**F**). Complete the stitch in the usual way.

Because the base of a relief stitch is below the top of the previous row, the stitch is shorter than its "normal" version. It is therefore necessary to reduce the length of the turning chain accordingly. A fabric made up of relief double-crochet stitches would use a turning chain of just two chains, rather than the usual three.

As the first row of relief stitches requires the stitches of the previous row to have sufficient height to be able to work around their stems, this foundation row needs to be tall. A fabric that used relief double-crochet stitches would normally be worked on to a foundation row of half double-crochet stitches.

Baby Blankets

Keep little ones cozy in their carriages and cribs with these soft pastel blankets.

MEASUREMENTS

Finished blanket is 29½ inches by 39½ inches.

MATERIALS

For striped blanket:

Sirdar Wash 'n' Wear Double Crepe (1¾ oz. per ball): 8 balls in first color (white), and 8 balls in second color (blue)

For plain blanket:

Sirdar Wash 'n' Wear Double Crepe (1¾ oz. per ball): 15 balls in yellow

For both blankets:

Size E crochet hook

GAUGE

20 sts and 11 rows to 4 inches measured over pattern using a size E hook, or size required to give correct gauge.

ABBREVIATIONS

rfdc = relief front double crochet worked as follows: work double crochet in usual way around stem of next st by inserting hook around stem of stitch from front and from right to left. See also page 11.

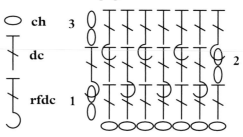

LEFT: In this stitch diagram the "hook" at the base of the double crochet stitch symbol signifies a relief stitch. Although all the relief stitches are relief front double crochets, the symbol is reversed for every other row as the direction of the work is also reversed.

STRIPED BLANKET

Center Section

Using a size E hook and first color, make 145 ch.

Foundation row: 1 dc into 3rd ch from hook, 1 dc into each ch to end, turn. 144 sts.

Row 1: 2 ch (counts as first st), * 1 rfdc around next st, 1 dc into next st, rep from * to last st, 1 rfdc around turning ch, turn. This row forms patt.

Work a further 7 rows in patt using first color.

**Break off first color and join in second color.

Using second color, work in patt for 8 rows.

Break off second color and join in first color.

Using first color, work in patt for 8 rows. Rep from ** 5 times more.

Break off first color and join in second color.

Work should measure 37¾ inches.

Edging

Using second color throughout, work edging as folls:

Round 1: 1 ch (does NOT count as st), now work 1 round of sc around all four edges, working 1 sc into each st across top of last row and across foundation ch edge, 3 sc into each corner point, and 3 sc into each pair of row end edges along sides, ending with ss to first sc, turn.

Round 2: 1 ch (does NOT count as st), 1 sc into each sc to end, working 3 sc into corner sc and ending with ss to first sc, turn.

Rounds 3 and 4: As round 2.

Now work 1 round of crab st (sc worked from left to right, instead of right to left) around entire outer edge, ending with ss to first st. Fasten off.

PLAIN BLANKET

Work as striped blanket but using same color throughout.

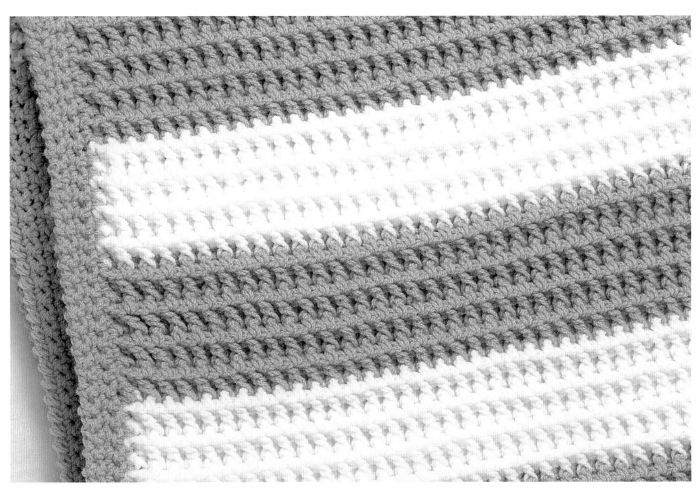

Filet Crochet

Filet crochet is the name given to a particular type of crochet that forms a mesh fabric made up of tiny open or solid crochet squares.

Filet crochet is worked following a chart that is an accurate diagram of what the finished piece will look like. The chart features solid blocks and open squares, arranged to form any type of design – geometric, floral, pictorial, or even words. The resulting fabric can be densely filled with a solid design, or very open creating a mesh with little design on it. (See chart below.)

Worked in a fine yarn, filet crochet generally uses just chain stitches and double crochets. The grid of the chart directly corresponds to the mesh of the crochet. Each row of squares on the chart becomes one row of the crochet. Each vertical line dividing the chart squares is worked as one double crochet stitch. Each horizontal line on the chart is a group of chain stitches.

Because the blocks of the crochet mesh should be true squares, each block is most often made up of three or four chains or double crochet stitches. There will be a double crochet at each side of the square, forming the vertical outline of the mesh, with either two chains or two double crochet stitches between, to either create the mesh or fill in the square. There are, of course, exceptions to this rule. Check the pattern you are following to make sure you know what size the mesh is supposed to be.

WORKING THE FILET MESH

1. Start a piece of filet crochet by making a foundation chain of the required length. This will be detailed in the pattern. Now work the first row of stitches that form the first row of squares by working into this chain.

2. To create a mesh fabric, work each square by working a double crochet at each side of the square and two chains to run across the

A

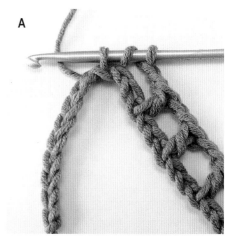

LEFT: This simple design, worked in filet crochet, is made up of solid blocks to form the heart motif on a mesh of open squares, with a border of solid squares. On this chart the solid squares are shown as a solid dot inside the square of the mesh, but you will sometimes find the solid square represented as a solid, filled-in black square. There are no details with the key to this diagram indicating how to work the mesh. You will need to refer to the instructions for this. The rows of the design are numbered at the beginning of each row.

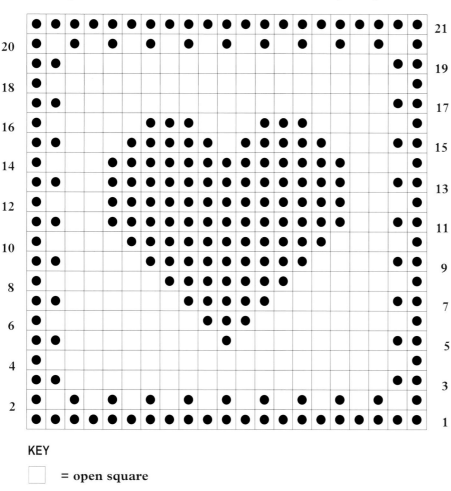

KEY

☐ = open square

● = solid block

top. The lower, fourth side of the square has already been formed by the foundation chain or, later on, by previous rows (**A**).

3. To fill in a square of the chart – to create a "block" – replace the two chain that would have formed the upper side of the square with two double crochet stitches worked into the chain running across the bottom of the square. The two double crochet stitches can either be worked into the chain stitches below them, or into the chain space (**B**). The effect created is very similar but working into the chain space is much easier.

Remember that at the beginning of a row of filet crochet there will be a turning chain. Once the double crochet has been worked at the end of one row, turn the work and work

the three chain that are needed to replace the double crochet that needs to sit at the beginning of the next row.

If the edge square of the design is an open square, you need to work an additional two chains to create the top of the square – a total of five chains. When working back over this open end square, remember to work the last double crochet into the third of these five chains. If the edge square of the design is a solid block, you will need to work the two double crochets that fill the block. If the square below is an open square, work these into the chain or chain space across the top. If the square below is a solid block, work one double crochet into each of the two double crochets that form the block below.

Although filet crochet is usually worked flat, in rows, it can be worked in rounds. Start each round in the same way as you would if

working a row, and close each round by working a slip stitch into the top of the three chain at the beginning of the round. Although there is no need to turn the work at the end of each round, when working a circular piece of filet crochet it is a good idea. The double crochets that form the vertical lines of the grid mesh tend to lean to one side slightly and, if all double crochets lean one way, the finished work will have a tendency to twist and bias.

Although most filet crochet designs are made up of simple open and solid squares, or "blocks," there are a few common variations.

LACETS AND BARS
Both of these design details usually appear together and fill two squares on the chart or mesh.

1. To work a lacet, start with a double crochet at the beginning of a square. Now replace the next two double crochet or chain stitches with a diagonal line of three chain stitches. Complete the "square" by working a single crochet into the point where the final double crochet should have been placed. To continue the lacet, work another diagonal line of three chain to replace the next two stitch-

es, and complete the lacet by working a double crochet into the normal place to form the last vertical side of the two squares. The resulting lacet forms a lacy "V" that sits over two squares of the mesh (**C**).

2. When working back over a lacet, it is necessary to work a bar that covers the top of both squares. A single open square will have a double crochet at each side and two chain across the top. For a double bar to cover a lacet, you will need to work five

chains at the center – two for each "square" and one to replace the missing center double crochet. Remember when working back over a bar that you will usually need to work a double crochet into the third of these five chains (**D**).

When following a chart for filet crochet, take time to read the key accompanying the chart, as well as any special abbreviations, so that you fully understand how the grid mesh is formed and how to work any details.

Lacy Curtain Panel

Hide an unsightly view with this pretty filet crochet panel set into a piece of sheer white fabric. Why not make a second panel and use it as a pretty tablecloth?

MEASUREMENTS

Finished panel is approx 20½ inches wide and 12 inches tall.

MATERIALS

Coats Aida 5 Crochet Cotton (1¾ oz. per ball): 2 balls in white
No. 5 steel hook

GAUGE

14 blocks and 17 rows to 4 inches using a No. 5 steel hook, or size required to give correct gauge.

ABBREVIATIONS

See page 11.

PANEL

Using a No. 5 steel hook, make 222 ch.

Row 1: 1 dc into 4th ch from hook, 1 dc into each ch to end, turn. 220 sts.

Row 2: 3 ch (counts as 1 dc), skip dc at end of last row, 1 dc into each of next 3 dc, *2 ch, skip 2 sts, 1 dc into next dc (this will now be called "1 open block"), 1 dc into each of next 3 sts (this will now be called "1 solid block"), rep from * to end, working last dc into top of turning ch, turn. 73 blocks.

Row 3: 3 ch (counts as 1 dc), skip dc at end of last row, 2 solid blocks, *1 open block, 1 solid block, rep from * to last block, 1 solid block, working last dc into top of turning ch, turn.

Row 4: 3 ch (counts as 1 dc), skip dc at end of last row, (1 solid block, 1 open block) twice, *1 solid block, 3 open blocks, rep from * to last 5 blocks, (1 solid block, 1 open

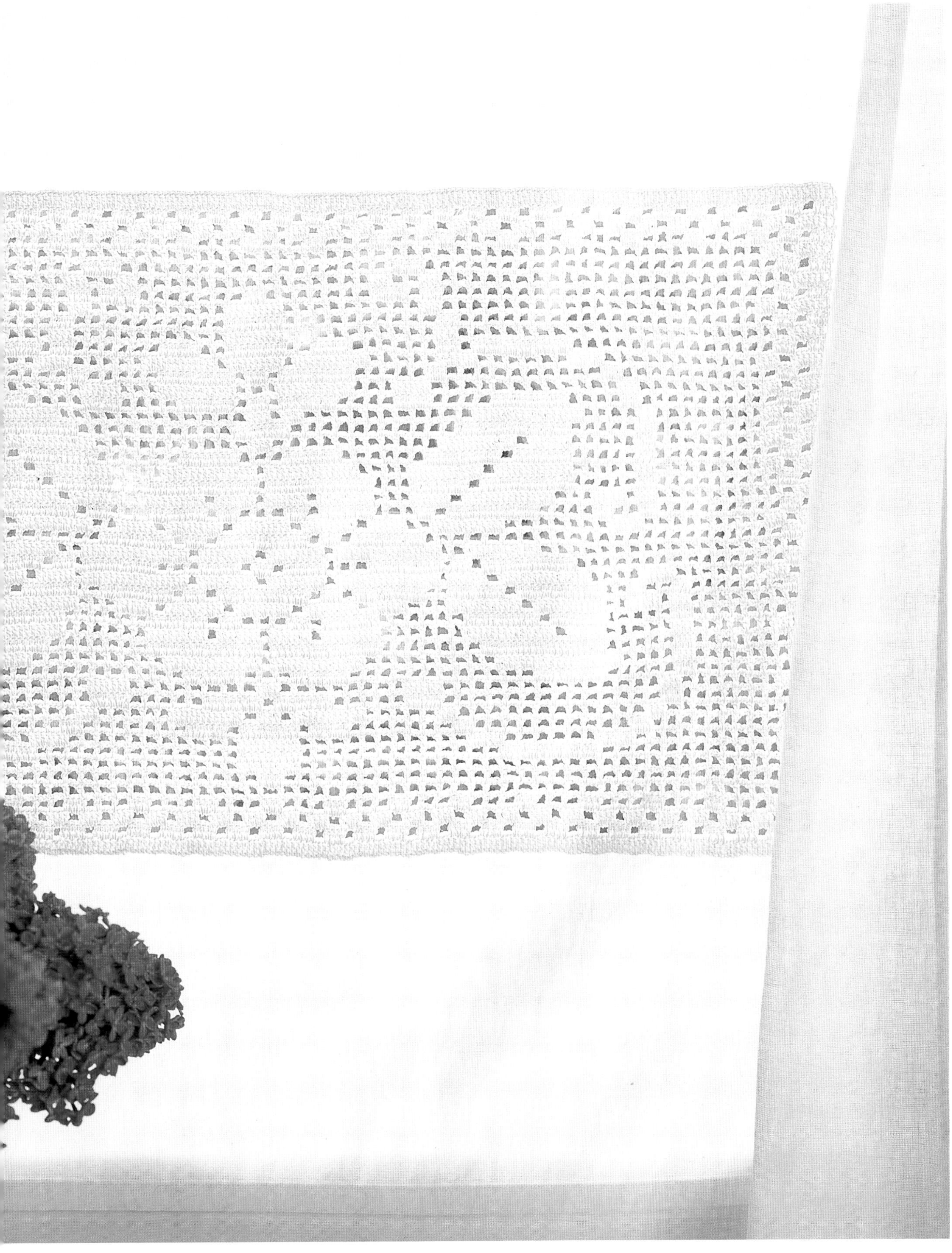

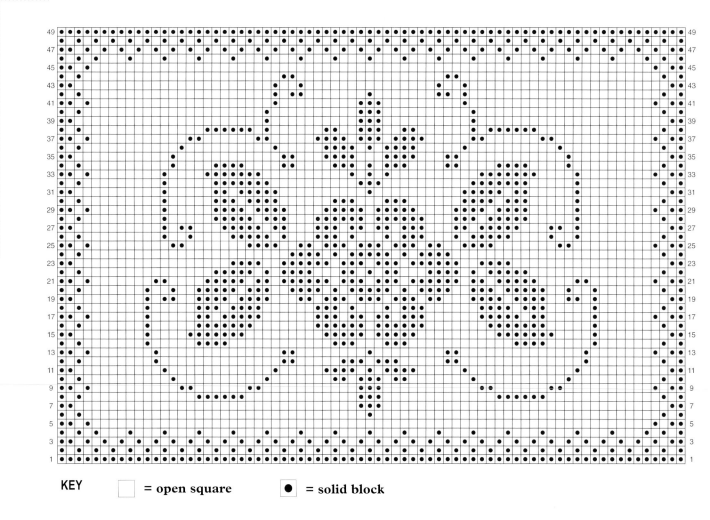

KEY ☐ = open square ● = solid block

block) twice, 1 solid block, turn.

Row 5: 3 ch (counts as 1 dc), 2 solid blocks, 1 open block, 1 solid block, 65 open blocks, 1 solid block, 1 open block, 2 solid blocks, turn.

Row 6: 3 ch (counts as 1 dc), 1 solid block, 1 open block, 1 solid block, 33 open blocks, 1 solid block, 33 open blocks, 1 solid block, 1 open block, 1 solid block, turn.

Row 7: 3 ch (counts as 1 dc), 2 solid blocks, 33 open blocks, 3 solid blocks, 33 open blocks, 2 solid blocks, turn.

Row 8: 3 ch (counts as 1 dc), 1 solid block, 1 open block, 1 solid block, 13 open blocks, 6 solid blocks, 13 open blocks, 3 solid blocks, 13 open blocks, 6 solid blocks, 13 open blocks, 1 solid block, 1 open block, 1 solid block, turn.

Row 9: 3 ch (counts as 1 dc), 2 solid blocks, 1 open block, 1 solid block, 10 open blocks, 2 solid blocks, 6 open blocks, 2 solid blocks, 11 open blocks, 3 solid blocks, 11 open blocks, 2 solid blocks, 6 open blocks, 2 solid

blocks, 10 open blocks, 1 solid block, 1 open block, 2 solid blocks, turn.

Row 10: 3 ch (counts as 1 dc), 1 solid block, 1 open block, 1 solid block, 10 open blocks, 1 solid block, 10 open blocks, 1 solid block, 7 open blocks, 2 solid blocks, 1 open block, 3 solid blocks, 1 open block, 2 solid blocks, 7 open blocks, 1 solid block, 10 open blocks, 1 solid block, 10 open blocks, 1 solid block, 1 open block, 1 solid block, turn.

These 10 rows set position of design.

Cont as now set, working from chart, until all 49 rows have been completed.

Fasten off.

Pin out to measurement given, cover with a damp cloth and leave to dry naturally.

Once dry, lay crochet panel onto right side of curtain in position required. Stitch in place using a narrow zigzag stitch worked over the finished edge and through the curtain fabric. Carefully trim away curtain fabric behind crochet panel and oversew the raw edges.

ABOVE: Follow this chart to work the design on the filet panel. Once the first 10 rows have been completed from the instructions, start by working row 11.

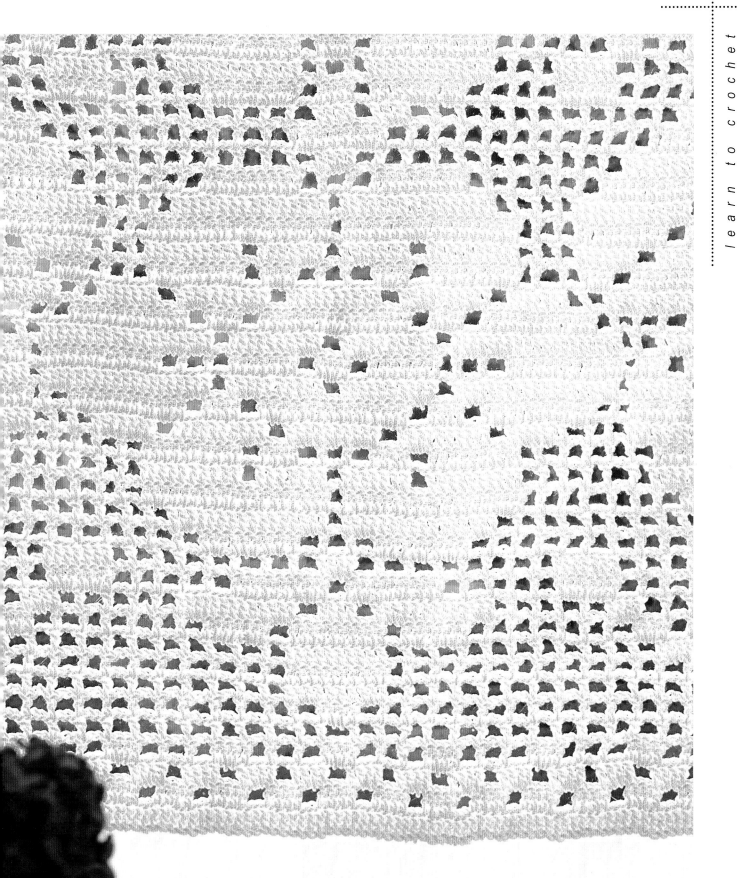

Resources

UNITED STATES

YARN AND OTHER SUPPLIES

Accordis Acrylic Fibers
15720 John J. Delaney Dr., Suite 204
Charlotte, NC 28277-2747
www.courtelle.com

Berroco, Inc
Elmdale Rd.
Uxbridge, MA 01569
(508) 278-2527

Boye Needle/Wrights
South St.
W. Warren, MA 01092
www.wrights.com

Brown Sheep Co., INC.
100662 County Rd. 16
Scottsbluff, NE 69361
(308) 635-2198

Cherry Tree Hill Yarn
52 Church St.
Barton, VT 05822
(802) 525-3311

Coats & Clark
Consumer Services
P.O. Box 12229
Greeneville, SC 29612-0224
(800) 648-1479
www.coatsandclark.com

Dale of Norway, Inc.
6W23390 Stonebridge Dr.,
Waukesha, WI 53186
(262) 544-1996

Elite Yarns
300 Jackson St.
Lowell, MA 01852
(978) 453-2837

Herrschners Inc.
2800 Hoover Rd.
Stevens Point, WI 54481
www.herrschners.com

JCA Inc.
35 Scales Lane
Townsend, MA 01469
(978) 597-3002

Lion Brand Yarn Co.
34 West 15th St.
New York, NY 10011
(212) 243-8995

Mountain Colors
4072 Eastside Hwy.
Stevensville, MT 59870
(406) 777-3377

Personal Threads
8025 West Dodge Rd.
Omaha, NE 68114
(800) 306-7733
www.personalthreads.com

Red Heart® Yarns
Two Lakepointe Plaza
4135 So. Stream Blvd.
Charlotte, NC 28217
www.coatsandclark.com

Rowan USA/Westminster Fibers, Inc.
4 Townsend West, Unit 8
Nashua, NH 03063
(603) 886-5041
www.knitrowan.com

Solutia/Acrilan® Fibers
320 Interstate N. Pkwy., Suite 500
Atlanta, GA 30339
www.thesmartyarns.com

TMA Yarns
206 W. 140th St.
Los Angeles, CA 90061

Trendsetter Yarns
16742 Stagg St.
Van Nuys, CA 91406
(818) 780-5497

Unique Kolours
23 North Bacton Hill Rd.
Malvern, PA 19355
(610) 280-7720

Yarns and ...
26440 Southfield Rd.
Lower Level #3
Lathrup Village, MI 48076-4551
(800) 520-YARN
www.yarns-and.com

ASSOCIATIONS

Association of Crafts & Creative Industries
1100-H Brandywine Blvd.
P.O. Box 3388
Zanesville, OH 43702-3388
(740) 452-4541

Craft Yarn Council of America
P.O. Box 9
Gastonia, NC 28053
Tel: 704-824-7838
www.craftyarncouncil.com

Crochet Guild of America
P.O. Box 127
Lockport, IL 60441
(877) 852-9190
www.crochet.org
www.cgoapresents.com

Hobby Industry Association
319 East 54th St.
Elmwood Park, NJ 07407
(201) 794-1133
www.hobby.org

The National Needlework Association
P.O. Box 3388
Zanesville, OH 43702-3388
(704) 455-6773
www.tnna.org

Society of Craft Designers
P.O. Box 3399
Zanesville, OH 43702-3388
(740) 452-4541

Western States Craft & Hobby Association
22033 Fries Ave.
Carson, CA 90745
(310) 549-5631

CANADA

Diamond Yarn of Canada Ltd.
155 Martin Ross Ave.
North York, ON M3J 2L9
(416) 736-6111
or
9697 St Laurent
Montréal, QC H3L 2N1
(514) 388-6188

S. R. Kertzer, Ltd.
105A Winges Rd.
Woodbridge, ON L4L 6C2
(800) 263-2354
www.kertzer.com

Koigu Wool Designs
RR1
Chatsworth, ON N0H 3H3
(519) 794-3066

Lily®
320 Livingston Ave. S.
Listowel, ON N4W 3H3
(519) 291-3780

Patons®
320 Livingstone Ave. S.
Listowel, ON N4W 3H3
www.patonsyarns.com

ASSOCIATIONS

Canada Craft & Hobby Association
#24 1410-40 Ave., NE
Calgary, AL T2E 6L1
(403) 291-0559

Canadian Crafts Federatopm
c/o Ontario Crafts Council
Designers Walk
170 Bedford Rd., Suite 300
Toronto, ON M5R 2K9
(416) 408-2294
www.canadiancraftsfederation.ca

Index

Acknowledgments

With thanks to the following people for all their help: Mrs Palmer, Julie Gill, Stella Smith, Kathleen Hargreaves, David Rawson, Ola Jankowska and Tricia McKenzie. I would also like to thank Rosemary Wilkinson and Clare Sayer at New Holland, and Shona Wood for her beautiful photographs.